Inside the
South African Reserve Bank
Its Origins and Secrets Exposed
by
Stephen Mitford Goodson

Inside the
South African Reserve Bank
Its Origins and Secrets Exposed
by
Stephen Mitford Goodson

Copyright © 2014 Black House Publishing Ltd

All rights reserved. No part of this book may be reproduced in any form by any electronic or mechanical means including photocopying, recording, or information storage and retrieval without permission in writing from the publisher.

ISBN-13: 978-0-9927365-8-3

Black House Publishing Ltd
Kemp House
152 City Road
London
UNITED KINGDOM
EC1V 2NX

www.blackhousepublishing.com
Email: info@blackhousepublishing.com

This book is dedicated to
His Imperial Majesty
Tsar Alexander II
who on 12 June 1860 established by ukase the
State Bank of the Russian Empire
the largest and most beneficent state bank
in the history of the world.

The main mark of modern governments is that we do not know who governs, *de facto* any more than *de jure*. We see the politician and not his backer, or what is most important of all, the *banker* of that backer. Throned above all, in a manner without parallel in all the past, is the veiled prophet of finance, swaying all men by some sort of magic.
– G. K. Chesterton

By the Same Author

General Jan Christian Smuts: The Debunking of a Myth

A History of Central Banking and the Enslavement of Mankind

Contents

Foreword	7
Introduction	13
Acronyms and Abbreviations	17

Chapter I

The Foundation of the South African Reserve Bank	19
Henry Strakosch	31

Chapter II

The South African Reserve Bank Bill of 1944	33
South African Reserve Bank Bill: House of Assembly	33
South African Reserve Bank Bill: The Senate	39

Chapter III

Director of South African Reserve Bank	51
Election as Non-Executive Director	51
South African Bank Note Company Ltd	59
Crane Currency	62
Nelson Mandela Bank Notes	63
South African Mint	64
Suspension	65

Chapter IV

Reserve Bank's "Holocaust" Revisionist	67
The "Holocaust"	69
Resignation	89

Chapter V

Defective Policies and Failures of the South African Reserve Bank	91
Fit And Proper Directors	91
Previous Scandals	93
Continuous Linked Settlement System	96
JP Morgan Chase & Co.	97
Where Is All The Gold?	101
Can The Bank of England Be Trusted?	103
Shareholder Dividends	105
Seigniorage	106
Academia	109
Sovereign Wealth Fund	114
Monetary Policy Committee	114
Independence	115

Inflation	117
UBUNTU Party	120

Chapter VI
The Solution: The State Bank of the Republic of South Africa   123

Appendix I
How Money is Created   131

Appendix II
Proposed Legislation   135

Appendix III
Frequently Asked Questions   145

Index   147

Inside the
South African Reserve Bank
Its Origins and Secrets Exposed
by
Stephen Mitford Goodson

Foreword

It isn't what we don't know that gives us trouble;
It is what we know that isn't so.
— Will Rogers

Once in a while a book comes along which completely shatters a commonly held view about an "institution" that is considered as the custodian of a country's monetary system by ensuring its economic health. Stephen Mitford Goodson has done the country a great favour by exploding this myth in his book, *Inside the South African Reserve Bank – Its Origins and Secrets Exposed*. His shattering exposition of the despicable and immoral activities of the South African Reserve Bank demonstrates tremendous courage. The tragedy of our times is that few people are willing to stand up for truth as Goodson has done in his book. This detrimental malaise is best noted in the words of Edmund Burke who said, "The only thing necessary for the triumph of evil is for good men to do nothing."

Speaking truth to power is not easy as people fear the repercussions that often follow. This is clearly evidenced in the actions of greedy money-lenders. They will do everything in their power to smear, malign and even persecute a whistle-blower so that people are distracted from the message that exposes their wrong-doing. For his efforts to expose the truth, Goodson has not escaped from persecution or getting his name maligned in the mainstream media.

One can cite numerous examples of people who were persecuted because they stood up for truth, righteousness and justice. The most notable example is that of Jesus Christ. Was he not persecuted for throwing out the greedy money-lenders from the synagogue? Were Mandela and Sisulu and a host of others who spoke out against apartheid not persecuted because they stood up for justice?

Foreword

During the apartheid period, a handful of citizens like, Bram Fischer and Beyers Naude, emerged from within the White community, who, despite the privileges accorded to them, exposed the deception of the government's brainwashing that apartheid was justified by the Bible. For exposing the truth, they became outcasts in their own community. The critical element which made it possible for the wider White community to be swayed by the government's indoctrination that the Black majority must be dispossessed, subjugated and oppressed, was "greed". That such a belief perverted Christianity was simply marginalised. That dispossessing the Black majority of their land and rights went against their own innate sense of righteousness was totally disregarded. Their "greed" dictated that they amass wealth even if it is at the expense of others and this became the driving focus to achieve their own covetous goal.

In this post-apartheid period, Stephen Goodson stands tall amongst those South African stalwarts like Nelson Mandela and Bram Fisher for standing up for righteousness and justice by exposing the nefarious monetary policies of the South African Reserve Bank. In this instance, it is the "greed" of the banks to accumulate wealth for themselves that is the driving force, regardless of who gets hurt in the process. Using practices which are both immoral and fraudulent, the banks have managed to gain the power to control the economy of the country. What is worse, the bank owners' greed to achieve this wealth at any expense has resulted in seriously exacerbating the poverty levels in the country to a point that many have to go to bed hungry.

Considering the billions the banks are able to create by their Fractional Reserve System and other reprehensible activities, their actions become both deplorable and unforgivable. It is these kinds of crimes which legitimise the increasing calls made by many to abolish the Reserve Bank in its present form as a private institution which is neither responsible nor accountable to either government or the people. Goodson's book offers an alternative beneficial model to the current avaricious one that is continually widening the gap between the rich and the poor.

By granting commercial banks the right to "create money out of nothing," the Reserve Bank allows the plutocrats to amass wealth which should rightfully belong to the people. That in this process innocent citizens are their primary victims is of little concern to the owners of the commercial banks. Their only concern is to ensure that the government and the country's citizens will be forever enslaved through perpetual debt. Through this means, the bank owners aim to achieve their "New World Order" agenda which is to dominate and control the governments around the world. This agenda is exposed by the highly esteemed historian, Professor Carroll Quigley of Georgetown University, who, as an insider, had intimate knowledge of the private bank owners' hidden agenda. He reveals:

> "The powers of financial capitalism had another far reaching aim, nothing less than to create a world system of financial control in private hands able to dominate the political system of each country and the economy of the world as a whole. This system was to be controlled in a feudalist fashion by the central banks of the world acting in concert, by secret agreements, arrived at in frequent private meetings and conferences. The apex of the system was the Bank for International Settlements in Basel, Switzerland; a private bank owned and controlled by the world's central banks which were themselves private corporations. The growth of financial capitalism made possible a centralization of world economic control and use of this power for the direct benefit of financiers and the indirect injury of all other economic groups."

Foreword

Any honest appraisal of the economic situation of most countries around the world would show that the bank owners have been very successful in accomplishing their hidden agenda to create that "financial control in private hands able to dominate the political system of each country." The impact of such enslavement, in the words of Reginald McKenna, Chairman of the Midland Bank, would be that, "those who control the credit of the nation direct the policy of Governments and hold in the hollow of their hands the destiny of the people." The consequences of such a situation would be dire for any nation as it would mean that any country which is beholden to the private bankers will never be truly free, independent or even democratic.

One of the merits of the book, *Inside the South African Reserve Bank – Its Origins and Secrets Exposed*, is that Goodson's exposure is presented from the point of view of an "insider," as both a shareholder and a former Director. Hence the information he provides must be taken seriously if citizens of South Africa wish to end their own enslavement. Failing this, the majority of South Africans will find themselves in the situation aptly described by President Thomas Jefferson of the United States who said in reference to the Second Bank of the United States that:

> "If the American people ever allow private banks to control the issue of their currency, first by inflation, then by deflation, the banks... will deprive the people of all property until their children wake-up homeless on the continent their fathers conquered... The issuing power should be taken from the banks and restored to the people, to whom it properly belongs."

Those reading *Inside the South African Reserve Bank – Its Origins and Secrets Exposed* with an open mind, will discover that one of the major outcomes Goodson wishes to achieve is the noble but just goal to bring about a nationalisation of the South African currency so that the creation of money and the issuing power of the currency is taken away from the banks and restored to the people and its government. This is the only way South Africans will be able to free themselves from perpetual enslavement to the greedy bank owners.

The choice facing one is stark but clear: A citizenry which remains in denial, will remain ignorant, and will unwittingly end up facilitating their own enslavement by the unscrupulous bankers. The power to bring about change is in the hands of informed citizens. This is so eloquently expressed by Margaret Mead who said:

> "Never doubt that a small group of thoughtful committed people, can change the world; indeed, it's the only thing that ever has."

Ahmed Motiar, B.A., M.Ed

4 July 2014

Introduction

This volume should be read in conjunction with *A History of Central Banking and the Enslavement of Mankind*[1], which describes the decisive role that central banks have been playing in the bribing of key legislators, counterfeiting the currency of enemy countries, fomenting wars and undermining the welfare and sovereignty of nations. The premier example is the Bank of England. Established 320 years ago, this bank provided the blueprint on which all other central banks have been modelled and is the benchmark of unlawful behaviour. All central banks are in essence criminal organisations, which prey on the ignorance of their subject peoples by allowing private banks to create money out of thin air and then charging endless amounts of interest on mortgages, and taxes to pay for the interest on the loans of government and state-owned institutions.

The South African Reserve Bank (SARB) is no exception in this regard, especially since it permitted Dr Nico Diederichs, former Minister of Finance and State President to loot the Treasury in the 1970s, by allocating to himself an unauthorised commission on all gold sales in Zürich, Switzerland, which in today's values would be the equivalent of over R1 billion. This venality reached unparalleled heights when corrupt SARB officials allowed crooked businessmen and politicians to ransack South Africa's foreign exchange reserves and strategic gold reserve of 3,000 tons in the 1980s and early 1990s.

The opening chapters on the history of the SARB reveal the valiant efforts of the Labour Party under the leadership of Colonel Frederic Creswell to set up a State Bank under the exclusive control of Parliament and the Treasury. Regrettably, outside influences prevented this

---

1   Black House Publishing, London, 2014, 214 pp.

Introduction

from happening. A distinguished economist and former Secretary for Finance, Dr J. E. Holloway, once described the monetary system run by the SARB and the commercial banks as a "colossal fraud".[2] In a private letter to the editor of the newsletter *Behind The News*, Ivor Benson, he wrote as follows:

> "It is not that governments do not know what sound money is. They do not want sound money, because they get the benefit from creating unearned money and exchanging this for earned goods and services thereby continually adding water to the milk and creating more inflation.
>
> "This is, of course, bound to lead to a collapse, and the difficulties they are now experiencing in devising a reformed monetary system will in time teach them that civilisation cannot endure on a basis of fraudulent money."[3]

Since 1994 the financial noose has tightened around South Africa's neck. 20 years of corruption, incompetence and misrule have brought the country to the brink of being declared a failed state. The path leading to the economic and social destruction of South Africa was unleashed on February 2, 1990 by former State President Frederik Willem de Klerk. In the process, the traitor De Klerk - and he has been preceded by a number of others - betrayed not only the Afrikaners, not only the people of European origin, but all the peoples of South Africa. For this treacherous conduct he was richly compensated. Four years ago, at a restaurant in Munich, Germany, De Klerk was heard boasting to some friends that he had an investment portfolio at Bank von Ernst, Liechtenstein, worth over

---

2   *Behind The News*, Pinetown, Natal, May 1977, 5.
3   Dr J.E. Holloway, Private letter to Ivor Benson, *Behind The News*, Krugersdorp, Transvaal, February 1979, 7.

one billion Swiss francs or almost R12 billion, and that he was this bank's biggest client. While De Klerk gloats over his ill-gotten gains, he appears to be a man without a conscience, oblivious to the fate of his own Afrikaner people, as 1,000,000 or ⅓ of all Afrikaners, many of whom are trained and qualified, have been reduced to living in squatter camps[4] or temporary accommodation, while many children suffer from undernourishment.

It seems that prior to 1994 from an economic perspective South Africans enjoyed "a better life for all" when unemployment for black people fluctuated between 5% and 10% per annum and the economy regularly achieved growth rates in GDP of between 6% and 8% per annum. This perspective has been endorsed by the Gini coefficient, a complicated algebraic formula which was devised by Italian statistician Corrado Gini in 1912 in order to calculate the distribution of income in different countries. It is recognised throughout the world as being an accurate measurement by such international bodies as the Organisation for Economic Co-operation and Development and the United Nations. In 1970 the ratio for all races in South Africa was .46 which is about the world average. To-day South Africa has the worst co-efficient at .70 in the world! This depressing fact is reflected in the 16 million welfare recipients, the 10% decline in life expectancy from 66 in 1994 to 59 to-day, 40% black employment,[5] 50% of the population living below the poverty datum line, the increase in government debt from R294 billion in 1994 to R1.4 trillion in 2014 and the 1.3 million taxpayers who pay 85% of all taxes and receive negligible benefits.

---

4   See http://www.censorbugbear.org/farmitracker/reports/view/2186?l=hu_HU for a BBC3 TV documentary which features the largest White squatter camp in South Africa at Coronation Park outside Pretoria. The camp does not have running water.

5   The trade union COSATU has estimated the black unemployment rate at 36%, while a University of South Africa study in July 2010 gave a figure of 40%.

Introduction

Although everyone has the vote,[6] it is evident that the "anti-apartheid struggle" was little more than a grotesque hoax used to seduce South Africa into the clutches of the international bankers' New World Order.

Now is the time for people of all races to join hands in the battle cry of Andrew Jackson, seventh president of the United States of America, which he issued 180 years ago on the subject of the Rothschild owned Second Bank of the United States.

> "You are a den of vipers and thieves. I have determined to rout you out and by the Eternal God, I will rout you out!"[7]

Stephen Mitford Goodson

June 2014

---

[6] The total potential voting population of South Africa is 32.6 million, of whom 25 million or 76.7 % are registered as voters. Of the latter total in the 2014 general election, 18.6 million or 74,4% voted, which means that 14 million or 42.9% of the population no longer have any interest in participating in the so called democratic process. The ANC's share of the total potential vote has slumped from an estimated 53% in 1994 to 35% or 11.4 million in 2014. This indicates that in terms of the overall potential voting population the ANC is a minority government.

[7] Andrew Jackson speaking to a group of bankers in Philadelphia in 1834. In 1836 President Jackson liquidated this foreign owned central bank and replaced it with an Independent Treasury System based on redeemable paper and specie.

Acronyms and Abbreviations

ANC	African National Congress
BIS	Bank for International Settlements
CEO	Chief Executive Officer
CIA	Central Intelligence Agency
CLSS	Continuous Linked Settlement System
CME	Chicago Mercantile Exchange
CSU	Christian Social Union.
GDP	Gross Domestic Product
HRH	His Royal Highness
IEC	Independent Electoral Commission
IMF	International Monetary Fund
M&G	Mail & Guardian
MPC	Monetary Policy Committee
NEDCOM	Non-Executive Directors' Committee
OGM	Ordinary General Meeting
PLC	Public Limited Company
RBA	Reserve Bank of Australia
RBN	Republic Broadcasting Network
SAAF	South African Air Force
SARB	South African Reserve Bank
SEC	Securities Exchange Commission
SWF	Sovereign Wealth Fund.
VAT	Value Added Tax
US 1$	= R10

General Jan Christian Smuts was Prime Minister (1919-1924) and (1939-1948). On the "advice" of the international bankers he introduced income tax and a central bank, thus ensuring the permanent enslavement of the South African people.

Chapter I

The Foundation of the South African Reserve Bank

The issue which has swept down the centuries and which will have to be fought sooner or later, is the people versus the banks.
  – Sir Alexander James Cockburn,
  Lord Chief Justice of England, 1875.

The Union of South Africa was the first victim after World War I to be singled out for the establishment of a central bank. General Smuts became Prime Minister, after succeeding General Louis Botha who after having contracted Spanish influenza had committed suicide by slashing his wrists on August 27, 1919.[1] Smuts had been appointed Minister of Finance in 1912, even though he "had never shown any financial ability...had no experience of business...his personal finances and his accounts were haphazard and usually neglected...he was useless in detail",[2] yet he was responsible for introducing the Income Tax Act in 1914. Income tax forms an integral part of the usury system and is first and foremost employed to defray the interest on government loans, which represent money which has been created out of nothing by private bankers.

Smuts was a supporter of what is today known as the New World Order and had been recruited during the time he was studying at Christ's College, Cambridge University (1891-93). In 1895 he became legal secretary and acolyte[3] of

---

1 P.J. Pretorius, *Volksverraad*, Libanon-Uitgewers, Mosselbaai, South Africa, 1996, 66.

2 H.C. Armstrong, *Grey Steel J.C. Smuts A Study in Arrogance*, Arthur Barkers Ltd, London, 1937, 272. See also S.M. Goodson, *General Jan Christian Smuts The Debunking of a Myth*, Bienedell Uitgewers, Pretoria, 2012, 22-24.

3 H.C. Armstrong, op.cit., 46.

The Foundation of the South African Reserve Bank

freemason[4] Cecil John Rhodes, although he would temper this enthusiasm, albeit temporarily, after the Jameson Raid in January 1896.

Smuts was a friend of Sir Henry (born Heinrich) Strakosch, a Moravian Jew[5] who later converted to High Anglicanism. Strakosch had previously worked for the Anglo-Austrian Bank of South Africa in the 1890s and in 1902 was appointed managing director of Union Corporation in London and later became chairman. Union Corporation was taken over by General Mining in 1980.

In 1919 Smuts consulted Strakosch about South Africa's loss of gold reserves as a result of the 23.1% devaluation of the pound sterling from $4.76 to $3.66 on March 20, 1919. This devaluation had resulted in the gold price increasing from £4 5s. to £6 7s. per fine ounce. Gold purchased in South Africa could be sold at a premium in London and this led to £2.9 million in gold coins leaving the country between April 1, 1918 and March 31, 1920. Furthermore South African commercial banks were compelled to buy gold at the higher price in order to have sufficient cover for the bank notes they issued. At that time the statutory requirement was that bank notes had to have a minimum gold cover of 40%. In order to counter these unfavourable trends, it was deemed advisable to establish a central bank, which would hold all the country's gold reserves.

Strakosch responded by writing a 34 page pamphlet divided into nine sections called *The South African Currency and Exchange Problem*[6] dated February 5, 1920. About ten years ago the author examined a copy of this document at the South

---

4   Member of the Apollo University Lodge, Oxford, England.
5   His mother was a Jewess, Mathilde Winterberg.
6   H. Strakosch, *The South African Currency and Exchange Problem*, Johannesburg, Central News Agency Limited, 1920. The pamphlet can now be viewed only in microfilm.

African Library in Cape Town. Aged to a brownish hue inside he found a large visiting card with Strakosch's London address and telephone number in the bottom left hand corner. No doubt he had generously donated this copy to the library. On pages 32-33 the case for a central bank is postulated as follows:

> "No one can study the experience of the great commercial nations without being impressed by the high efficiency of their credit organisations. The work of the great central banking institutions in piloting them through prosperity and adversity is especially noteworthy. The experience of these countries with their centuries of economic life, where every financial problem receives careful and intelligent consideration and where vast financial transactions are constantly taking place, should certainly be suggestive and valuable to us. If we are to profit by their experience, the question of establishing a Central Reserve Bank for the Union should receive the closest attention."[7]

"The study the writer has been able to give to the subject has led him to the conclusion that the system which will probably be found to be best suited to this country is one which in its fundamental principles follows that of the Federal Reserve System of the United States of America."[8]

"The Federal Reserve System of America has been modelled to a very considerable extent, on the lines of the old established systems of the principal continental countries of Europe, and has stood the test of adversity by successfully seeing the country through the difficult times of the great war. It is doubtful whether a better model can be found."[9]

---

7   Ibid., 32-33.
8   Ibid., 33.
9   Ibid., 34.

The Foundation of the South African Reserve Bank

Strakosch's tendentious praise of the "great central banking institutions", which have "stood the test of adversity" and his recommendation that a central bank be modelled on the US Federal Reserve Bank is filled with hypocrisy and cant. His "study" of central banking had presumably not included the Bank of England, which failed to serve the interests of the English people since its inception in 1694 and more particularly after Nathan Rothschild seized control of it in 1815[10]. On the basis of these few paragraphs of sciolism, South Africa would be condemned to permanent slavery.

A Select Committee, consisting of five members of the ruling South African Party, two from the National Party, two from the Union Party and one from the Labour Party, considered the Currency and Banking Bill, the Strakosch pamphlet, the minutes of the Gold Conference held in Pretoria in October 1919 and the minutes of the Committee on Currency and Banking.

This committee was criticised by John William Jagger of the Union Party, who wanted to know why "no one was appointed who had expert knowledge of a subject which was one of the most intricate and important ever brought before Parliament" and he wondered furthermore "if all committees were appointed on such a basis."[11] He was perturbed that "upon the advice of men who have no special knowledge and who before the inquiry took place had given no special attention to the matter"[12] now expected Parliament to adopt a bill, which was "of the most vital importance to this country."[13]

Great unease was expressed by members of all parties,

---

10 See S. M. Goodson, *A History of Central Banking and the Enslavement of Mankind*, Black House Publishing Ltd, London, 2014, Chapter II, The Hidden Origins of the Bank of England, 21-46.

11 *Cape Times*, July 16, 1920.

12 Ibid.

13 Ibid.

Inside the South African Reserve Bank

General Hertzog was Prime Minister (1924-1939) and during his term of office always put South Africa first. His proposal in 1920 that the Banking and Currency Bill be referred to a commission of enquiry for two years was rejected.

which was typified by the comments of John X Merriman of the South African Party, who said that "he could not conceive anything more detrimental and more foolish than to try and force a bill like this through before the people of the country had had an opportunity of studying it, reading it or knowing anything about it."[14]

Mr Jagger wished to know why it was necessary "to rush the bill through this session, as the measure was an extremely important one, and would affect every inhabitant of the Union."[15] He found that the report of Colonel Frederic Hugh Page Creswell of the Labour Party, which proposed a State Bank "showed a far better grip of their question, and was an abler document than the Committee report itself."[16] He also said that the proposal for a central reserve bank "had not been an entire success in the country of its origin – the United States."[17]

Strakosch came under persistent criticism for being a foreigner, who had no knowledge of South African banking and economic conditions. Frederick William Beyers of the National Party observed that there was "no doubt that a number of members had placed Strakosch on a pedestal which, naturally, greatly detracted from the value of the Committee's finding."[18] James Wellwood Mushet of the Union Party reached the heart of the matter when he said that "the man who had the last word with the committee was Mr Strakosch. His experience of experts was that no people in the world differed as they did. They had got Mr Strakosch with his six books of Euclid coming before the committee and making them swallow the whole lot in nine lessons."[19]

---

14   *Cape Times*, July 6, 1920.
15   Ibid.
16   Ibid.
17   Between 1820 and 1910 the US dollar retained its purchasing power. In 1920 six years after the US Federal Reserve Bank had been in operation, the dollar depreciated in value by 56.1%.
18   *Cape Times*, July 20, 1920.
19   Ibid. Euclid was a Greek mathematician also known as the "Father of

It was only the Labour Party which was fully apprised of what was at stake and the contributions of three of their members are given in full.

"Mr Frank Nettleton (Labour Party, Umbilo) said he was not so much concerned with what the Government wished to do as with what they did not wish to do. He referred to the establishment of a State Bank. He conceded that it was waste of time to chop off the bad branches of a tree instead of taking up the tree by the roots. The banks had been the factor in the enslavement of the workers, and as they merely existed to loan great enterprises at exorbitant interest they must be inimicable to the good of the people as a whole. He thought it was time Ministers of Finance all over the world considered the establishment of State Banks. The present measure was going to establish the banks of South Africa on a stronger footing than ever, and he thought it was for the House to consider whether they should not scrap the present proposals and construct a practical scheme for a State Bank. He did not attach much value to experts, for they had brought the world into a mess. What asses we were to allow our wealth to get into the hands of private banks, instead of having a State Bank of our own. The Australian State Bank had saved Australia 23 millions. The currency problem was the result of the capitalistic system."[20]

"Mr Creswell (Labour Party, Troyeville) said that Mr Burton [Minister of Finance], in his opening statement about the bill, gave the impression that all members of the Committee met with open minds on this subject, and had no preconceived ideas with regard to it. So far as he was concerned that was not the case, however. He had

---

Geometry". The nine lessons possibly refer to the nine sections of Strakosch's pamphlet.

20 *Cape Times*, July 17, 1920.

some ideas upon it, and so had every other member of the Committee, and he believed no one had clearer ideas or views in his mind than the Minister himself. The measures proposed were measures the Government had carefully prepared, and he affirmed all the way through from the first week during which the Committee sat he had not the faintest doubt that the Minister had in his mind the nature of the report by which he would bring out those ideas. It was therefore, rubbish for the Minister to say that he went into Committee with an open mind and no powers at all and he affirmed that the Minister was from the first a sincere disciple of the Strakosch idea."[21]

"Mr Creswell said that the question of a State Bank had never been thrashed out, but had been dismissed without argument. He asked why they should not have a State Bank, and what evil was to be apprehended. There were he said, the most powerful reasons, in dealing with the question why it was time to examine impartially whether the interests of the country would not be best served by setting up a State Bank. The Central Reserve Bank was going to be dominated by the banking and financial interests of the country...Was it a sound thing to do, leaving the whole of the banking interests in private hands? The Central Bank was going to govern the country and the financial policy of the Minister. Their South African Ministers, he considered, had not devoted a great deal of research into questions of financial statesmanship, but expressed the views of the controllers of private enterprise. They wanted to see the big financial forces trained and controlled to do the work of the country by those who represented the people of the country. They could finance such a bank, and it was in the power of Parliament to direct that there should be a National Bank."[22]

---

21   Ibid.
22   *Cape Times*, July 27, 1920.

"Mr Walter Bayley Madeley (Labour Party, Benoni) said that when the House rose the previous night he was dealing with the amendment of his party and was protesting on the silence so far as debate was concerned, with which it was received. He could not recall any time when the question of the establishment or otherwise, of a State Bank had been fully debated or thoroughly thrashed out. All that had ever happened was what had happened on the present occasion, viz. that all those who were in opposition to the deal had never had the hardihood to attack it on its merits, being in the House in the interests of private enterprise, they dared not attack the arguments of amendments of his party on their merits. The Minister had trotted out the argument as to there being no precedents. But as a matter of fact there was one precedent in the form of the State Bank of Australia, which had been successful from the financial point of view. The speaker proceeded to instance the low cost at which the Australian State Bank could float loans compared to other countries. He wished the Minister would inform the House what the flotation of loans cost this country during the past few years.[23] The Australian could do it at 4/6 per centum. If the Minister would not go according to the Australian precedent, why did he go according to the American one? What had been done in the USA was not in the interests of the public, but of the banks. He demanded that the Government should keep a grip on the finances of the country by instituting a State Bank."[24]

It appears that there was a deliberate strategy to rush the bill through at the tail end of the parliamentary session, so as to give members as little time as possible to study it.

---

23 Interest of 5% was paid on Union Government Loan Stock compared to ⅔rds of one percent charged by the state bank of Australia, the Commonwealth Bank of Australia.

24 *Cape Times*, July 28, 1920.

The Foundation of the South African Reserve Bank

Sensible proposals by Mr Jagger that the bill only "be read a first time, but should not be pushed through this session so that Parliament and the country might have an opportunity of considering the matter"[25] and by General J.B.M. Hertzog, the leader of the National Party, that a commission of enquiry be appointed to deliberate over the matter for two years, were arrogantly brushed aside by the Minister of Finance.

On January 22, 1886 Adolf Heinrich Wilhelm von Scholz Secretary for the Treasury of Germany and for the Kingdom of Prussia (1882-1890) said that "**it would constitute an act of treason to sign away the independence of a state in reference to money**".[26]

A.N. Field expands on this vitally important matter as follows:

> "Nor can we escape the fact that a State in preferring the interests of the money power to those of the people comes dangerously near to an abnegation of sovereignty. A Government accepting a position in which a body of its private citizens announce terms on which they are 'willing to co-operate' with it – as financiers have done in some countries – has virtually ceased to be a Government. Accepting such a position, it becomes a mere front, a facade behind which these private persons rule the country. So far as it serves the people at all it fills the office, not of governing, but of mediating. The seat of sovereignty must be sought elsewhere."[27]

On August 2, 1920, 69 members of parliament unwittingly

---

25   *Cape Times*, July 6, 1920.
26   *The Times*, February 1886.
27   A.N. Field, *The Truth About The Slump - What the News Never Tells*, Privately published, Nelson, New Zealand, 1935, 189-190.

Inside the South African Reserve Bank

committed treason by voting for the Banking and Currency Bill and condemning South Africa to debt slavery in perpetuity. The 19 Labour Party members plus three Nationalists voted against the bill.

Finally, it may be noted that after the bank was founded, Governor Montagu Norman informed the Committee of Treasury in the Bank of England that "the policy and methods of the new bank should from the outset accord with those of the Bank of England."[28] Norman thereafter kept in close contact with his former chief accountant, William Clegg, the first governor of the SARB. The SARB was thus placed under constant surveillance in order to ensure that it did not deviate from the exploitative paradigm of usury.[29]

---

28   R.S. Sayers, *The Bank of England 1891-1944*, Cambridge, Cambridge University Press, 1976, 209.

29   In a similar fashion Hjalmar Schacht, president of the Reichsbank provided Montagu Norman with a constant stream of information about the activities of the Reichsbank and the state of the German economy.

Jewish banker and financier Henry Strakosch paid Winston Churchill's debts in exchange for Churchill spearheading International Jewry's campaign that sought a war with Germany, and the destruction of National Socialism's usury free banking system.

Henry Strakosch

From 1925-26 Strakosch served on the Royal Commission on Indian Currency and Finance, whose recommendation resulted in the establishment of the Reserve Bank of India on April 1, 1935.

In the 1930s while Winston Churchill was out of office and quite often spent time in sanatoriums recovering from alcoholic binges, he ran into financial difficulties because of his gambling debts and after his stock exchange investments had failed. On March 26, 1936, he had one week in which to settle his debts or lose his treasured home "Chartwell" in Kent.[30] Strakosch stepped into the breach and paid Churchill's debts. Churchill's tone changed dramatically from the frank and independent one of the 1920s to being servile towards "other interests". Strakosch would feed Churchill with exaggerated and often spurious statistics[31] regarding German rearmament in order to promote a war psychosis. In November 1936, Churchill informed US Brigadier General Robert E. Wood that "Germany is getting too strong, we must smash her."[32] Churchill became a bitter enemy of Germany, which had largely abandoned the fraudulent system of usury and reorganised the Reichsbank on state banking lines, in order to serve the needs of all Germany's people.

Strakosch died in London on October 30, 1943 and in his will dated August 27, 1941 he expunged Churchill's debt of £18,162. He also left a further £25,000[33] to Churchill and

---

30 D. Irving, *Churchill's War, The Struggle for Power,* Veritas Publishing Company Pty Ltd, Bullsbrook, Western Australia, 1987, 104.

31 W.S. Churchill, The Second World War, *The Gathering Storm,* Vol. 1, Cassell & Co. Ltd, London, 1948, 193 and D. Irving, op.cit., 49.

32 H.E. Barnes, Winston Spencer Churchill: A Tribute, *The Journal of Historical Review,* Summer 1980, Vol., No. 1, 163-165.

33 Last Will and Testament of Sir Henry Strakosch. According to the Bank of England's Inflation Calculator http://www.bankofengland.co.uk/education/inflation/index.htm £18,162 were worth £1,086,995, £25,000 were worth

Henry Strakosch

£10,000 to Smuts, stating in the case of the latter bequest that it was "as a token of friendship and gratitude reposed in me in connection with the several tasks he has entrusted to me."[34] These were the only major bequests. In such a manner are "friends" rewarded for past services rendered.

£965,322 and £10,000 were worth £386,129 respectively in 2012.

34   Last Will and Testament op.cit., 7-8.

Chapter II

The South African Reserve Bank Bill of 1944

Once a nation parts with the control of its credit and money, it matters not who makes the nation's laws. Usury, once in control, will wreck[1] any nation. Until the control of the issuance of currency and credit is restored to government, and recognized as its most sacred responsibility, all talk of sovereignty, of parliament, and of democracy, is idle and futile.[2]
- William Lyon Mackenzie King, Prime Minister of Canada.

South African Reserve Bank Bill: House of Assembly

On April 21, 1944 Jan Hendrik Hofmeyr,[3] Minister of Finance,[4] introduced the South African Reserve Bank Bill, which had become necessary in view of the fact that the Bank's 25 year old exclusive right to print bank notes was due to expire the following year. He said that the bank had been in the "nature of an experimental venture"[5] and that was why only a "probationary period" had been granted

---

1   In 2009 while travelling to Johannesburg the author sat next to Pallo Jordan, then Minister of Culture. In conversation the author mentioned that he was going to attend a Board meeting of the SARB. He replied, "So you are the people who are wrecking the economy."

2   During Mackenzie King's third term of office (1935-48) the government owned Bank of Canada operated as a state bank, issuing at one stage almost all of Canada's credit at a nominal interest charge.

3   He was the nephew of Jan Hendrik Hofmeyr, "Onze Jan", leader of the Afrikander Bond, which represented the interests of Afrikaners living in the then Cape Colony.

4   On account of his penchant for raising taxes, J. H. Hofmeyr was also known as "Jan Taks."

5   House of Assembly Debates, April 21, 1944, 5615.

and that it should now be placed on a more "permanent footing".[6] Furthermore he wished to "make it clear that it [was] not designed to compete with commercial banks and other financial institutions in their appropriate field of operations. After all, what we expect of the Reserve Bank is that it should on the one hand maintain a sound currency position and on the other hand control credit necessary in the interest of the national welfare and stability generally."[7] As will be described in greater detail in Chapter V, throughout the 93 years of its existence the Reserve Bank has failed to provide the country with a "sound currency" and "stability", principally because it is not responsible for creating the money supply free of debt and interest, which was formerly created out of cheque book money and is created currently mainly out of electronic money.

Mr Albertus Werth, the National Party member for George, pointed out that "this legislation places this tremendous power of life and death over the economic life of the people into private hands – a tremendous weapon for good or evil."[8] He also said that New Zealand had bought out its private shareholders as too had Canada in 1938 and wanted to know why South Africa "is the only one to stick to antiquated legislation."[9]

He thus proposed the following amendment which read as follows: "To omit all the words after 'That' and to substitute 'the Order for the Second reading be discharged and the subject of the bill be referred to a select committee for enquiry and report, with instructions to make such amendments that the state shall have full and effective control over the monetary and credit system of the country;

---

6   Ibid., 5620.
7   Ibid., 5617.
8   Ibid., 5623.
9   Ibid., 5624.

the Committee to have power to take evidence and call for papers and to have leave to bring up an amended bill.'"[10]

The amendment was defeated by 68 votes to 29.

The Minister of Finance admitted that "the commercial banks create credit"[11], but rejected the proposal of the National Party member for Krugersdorp, Mr Marthinus van den Berg, that the "Reserve Bank should be the only credit-giving institution."[12]

During the third reading of the bill Mr Werth emphasised how important it was not to leave the creation of sufficient credit in private hands and that the State should be responsible for "the provision of sufficient credit in the country to cause the machinery of commerce and industries to act smoothly, to regulate the provision of credit in such a manner that we are not going to have a boom period at one moment and a depression at the next."[13] He also expressed his fear that "owing to its lack of power of control, the Government will be powerless if these elements controlling huge financial resources should conspire in this country."[14] This is precisely what happened in 1985 when Gavin Relly, the chairman of Anglo American Corporation, and Willard C. Butcher the CEO of the Rockefeller controlled Chase Manhattan Bank, conspired to bring about the downfall of the South African government. Chase Manhattan abruptly refused to roll over the country's short term foreign loans amounting to $24 billion[15] and with the complicity of the US

---

10   Ibid., 5623.
11   April 25, 1944, 5748.
12   Ibid., 5749.
13   May 3, 1944, 6419.
14   Ibid., 6420.
15   R72 billion (R1 = $0.33).

Federal Reserve Bank demanded immediate repayment.[16] As a result of this unforeseen attack on the Reserve Bank, it was thrown into "total confusion" and was unable to respond in a coherent and effective manner. Eventually a debt standstill was negotiated.

On May 3, 1944 Mr John Christie, the Labour Party member for South Rand, said that the opportunity should be grasped to set up a national bank and that it was the most "logical thing to have done, to have come forward at this period of our history, to have put our finances, our control of credit, our entire financial credit, over every industry, control over every commercial activity, control over our post-war conditions, in the hands of a sound, solid banking law, that would enable us to meet every post-war difficulty without any trouble."[17] He also said that by not taking "real control of our banking and credit system"[18] a "terrible blunder"[19] was being committed. He strongly objected to the fact that private banks create money out of nothing as loans and then "can take from the great mass of people, from the industrialist, from commercial and other people, sums of money to pay for these overdrafts [i.e. interest], when the State can do that easily and so much more cheaply, and incidentally that private banks are using the credit of the State when they are using that money."[20] He also explained that what was at stake was not how the banking system should work, but rather "it is a question of who shall govern the country, whether the elected representatives of the people or the private banking interests."[21]

---

16 *Aida Parker Newsletter*, Johannesburg, Issue No. 70, November 19, 1985, 1 & 6.
17 May 3, 1944, 6431.
18 Ibid., 6432.
19 Ibid., 6432.
20 Ibid., 6433.
21 Ibid., 6433.

Inside the South African Reserve Bank

Mr Duncan Burnside, the Labour Party member for Fordsburg, who considered the proposed bill to be a "retrograde step"[22] condemned the privately owned banking system for having ruined the South African economy. He said that the investor was "at the mercy of the banking institution – I think I can call it the banking racket without any exaggeration. The industrialist and the commercial people are at the mercy of the banking racket just the same as the ordinary man in the street is. The banks have been known to ruin an industry completely in one fell swoop in their own interests. They have deprived that industry of the capital it possessed, and in the course of that they have of course deprived the workers of the work they should get."[23]

He was highly critical of the foolishness, which the Reserve Bank and its then Governor, Dr J. Postmus, had evinced in clinging to the gold standard[24] stating that "This existing Reserve Bank was the bank which agreed with the policy [of restricting credit] then adumbrated, and this existing Reserve Bank was the bank which through the medium of their governor prevented South Africa from leaving the gold standard. This existing Reserve Bank was the bank which through the medium of their governor had the audacity to tell this House that on questions of banking they were supreme."[25] This was indeed the case. Parliament was compelled to pass special legislation viz. the Currency and Exchanges Act of 1933 in order to force the Reserve Bank to take South Africa off the gold standard. This legislation was retroactively passed as the date on which South Africa left the gold standard was September 21, 1931.

---

22 Ibid., 6444.
23 Ibid., 6438.
24 For an incisive dissertation on the fallacy of the gold standard see A. Kitson, *A Fraudulent Standard*, Omni Publications, Hawthorne, California, (first published in 1917), 1972. He describes the gold standard as being "legalized fraud, a deception and a snare!", viii.
25 May 3, 1944, 6439.

The Reserve Bank, then as now, and so emphatically expressed by Mr Burnside, has always worked in the interests of the private banking sector to the detriment of the general population. The myth that it "acts as the Government desires"[26] could not be "further from the truth."[27] Finally, Mr Burnside alluded to the probability "that this bloody war in which we are now engaged and most certainly the last war, are more to be traced to the machinations of banking finances than to any single thing."[28]

Mr Alexander Wanless, the Labour Party member for Durban (Umbilo), expressed his desire "to find money for the expansion of industry through a State bank, and that such money should be provided free of interest. Money should be provided for Government purposes absolutely free of interest, though, of course, a charge must be made for their service. Whatever the bank has to pay by way of wages and so forth must be secured by charging a fee, but the money should be provided to the Government entirely free of interest and not only that – money should also be made available to provincial councils and municipalities, who should also be privileged to go to the State bank and get the money on the same terms and conditions. This is the important feature of it. If the Government wants money it raises it on a planned budget. In a planned budget you have the guarantee that the money so created will be used on essential things, and that is the best guarantee that there won't be any such thing as inflation, that is the ingredient which guarantees you against inflation. It guarantees a policy of expansion so that you can go on and produce the goods which the country is capable of producing and guarantees also the means for the consumption of these goods. In general, the people at large are beginning to

---

26   Ibid., 6440.
27   Ibid., 6440.
28   Ibid., 6440.

fasten on to the fantastic idea that bankers do create money out of nothing. The more that idea passes into the minds of the people of South Africa and other countries, the more will the demands increase on Parliament and the elected representatives of the people to get on with the job of seeing that this money created out of the credit of the country, is money which belongs to the country, and should not be allowed to remain in the hands of the bankers to charge interest on."[29] The third reading of the bill was passed by 68 votes to 23.

South African Reserve Bank Bill: The Senate

The following day on May 4, 1944 the Reserve Bank bill was referred to the Senate. Leading the debate in opposition[30] to the bill was Senator Sidney Smith of the Labour Party. Senator Smith had been elected to the Durban City Council at the age of 21 and later became Mayor of Durban (1945-1946). He was one of the most knowledgeable men on banking in the country at that time.

In his first speech he said that the bill was distinguished not for what it contained, but for what it omitted. He pointed out that the prestige which the Reserve Bank had obtained, was in reality the prestige which had been conferred by other financial institutions and he doubted whether it had much prestige amongst 80% of the population, who were "suffering from slow starvation."[31] He noted the failure of the bank to "wield its powers in the interest of equating the finances of the country with its productive capacity"[32] and the fact that "the Governor downwards, shall be

---

29 Ibid., 6447.
30 The Labour Party was in alliance with the ruling United Party.
31 Senate, May 4, 1944, 1986.
32 Ibid., 1986.

a person of what is called tested banking experience; in other words, orthodox bankers; in other words exponents of scarcity economics, who have no concern whatever with the point of whether a country can from an economic point of view maintain its people and produce enough goods to keep its people in a state of proper nourishment. They are concerned entirely with the question of treating money as a merchandise and increasing its value or lowering its value in relation to goods in just the manner that it likes."[33]

Senator Smith proposed an amendment to the bill which would authorise the government to issue fiduciary notes free of interest. He wished to replicate the fiduciary notes issue in Great Britain, where the House of Commons had recently authorised £1.15 billion of notes, which were not backed by gold, but by state securities. This monetary asset would not create inflation as it would immediately be deployed in productive activities. As a precedent he cited bank notes and coins, which have always been printed and coined as monetary assets free of interest in South Africa[34] since 1922 and 1923 respectively.

He said that the policy of the orthodox bankers for the past 300 years had been a "ghastly failure"[35] and all that was preventing the "realisation of an age of plenty is a rotten, antiquated, faulty financial system."[36] He then quoted from a speech made by one of the world's greatest champions of freedom, Abraham Lincoln.

> "Money is the creature of law and the creation of the original issue of money should be maintained as an exclusive monopoly of the National Government. Such needs can be

---

33   Ibid., 1987.
34   Ibid., 1989-2005.
35   Ibid., 1995.
36   Ibid., 1993.

served by issuing national currency and credit through the operation of a national banking system. The Government should create, issue and circulate all the currency and credit needed to satisfy spending power of the Government and the buying power of consumers. The privilege of creating and issuing money is not only the supreme prerogative of the Government, but it is Government's greatest creative opportunity. The people can and will be furnished with a currency as safe as their own Government. Money will cease to be the master and will become the servant of humanity. Democracy will rise superior to the money power."[37]

The amendment for the issue of fiduciary money was negated.

During the committee stage clause 8 of the Bill, which defined the powers and duties of the Bank was debated. Senator Smith said that the sub-clause which enabled the Bank to create additional money by the sale of gilt-edged securities was "a very clumsy process at the best of times"[38] and that it took "a very long time before that money [can] possibly filter through to the masses who need it."[39] He also demanded an explanation from the Minister of Finance as to why "the Reserve Bank failed in its duty in 1934-35-36 when there was dire distress in South Africa by reason of an insufficient flow of credit."[40] The Minister was unable to provide an answer.

Senator Smith also asked the Minister to explain the source of increase in the money supply by £200 million from 1936 to 1944. The Minister, a classicist by training, displayed his illiteracy of financial matters, when he claimed that

---

37   Ibid., 1996.
38   May 5, 1944, 2011.
39   Ibid., 2012.
40   Ibid., 2018.

the increased price of gold and a reduction in the level of imports had been responsible for this increase in the money supply. Obviously the £200 million could only have emanated from the commercial banks, which had created it out of nothing. This example of a lack of understanding, as to how the financial system functions, is typical of ministers of finance South Africa has been burdened with throughout its history.

During the third reading of the bill Senator Charles Lowe Henderson of the Labour Party stated that "the banks are the greatest racketeers the world has ever seen."[41] He referred to the failure of the Reserve Bank to avert "the awful tragedy of what is called depression"[42] and the likelihood of there being "further depressions in the future."[43] He also wanted to know how "as a result of the depression, the Reserve Bank lost all its reserves and half its capital."[44] He said that "there was any amount of material for production; there was any amount of labour to produce; there were people anxious to buy, but there was something wrong in between, and that was the currency and credit of South Africa. The flow must have been stopped by someone. I say it was the banks that control the world. I say advisedly it was and is the banks that rule the world."[45]

Senator Henderson then covered recent developments in other Commonwealth countries. He explained how the bankers brought down the Labour government of British Prime Minister Ramsay MacDonald "with a crash"[46] because the banks would "not accede to their requests"[47]

---

41 Ibid., 2029.
42 Ibid., 2029.
43 Ibid., 2029.
44 Ibid., 2029.
45 Ibid., 2030.
46 Ibid., 2031.
47 Ibid., 2031.

and therefore denied them "all sorts of [loan] facilities."[48] He said that this disgraceful behaviour of the bankers reinforced "the statement by many eminent economists that the man who controls the money controls the nation."[49]

He said that the prime minister of Canada, Mackenzie King, supported the establishment of a State bank and had much praise for the New Zealand Minister of Finance, Mr Walter Nash, who "has been one of the strongest advocates of the State banking system."[50] Below is a synopsis of the financial policy implemented by the Labour government of New Zealand, which brought about a rapid recovery in the economy. Senator Henderson said that New Zealand had "developed a system which is the envy of the world."[51]

New Zealand's agricultural exports of meat, wool and dairy products, which were badly affected by the Great Depression, were in 1935 down by 40% compared to five years previously. There was much poverty and the unemployment rate rose to 27%. Many home owners lost their properties as they were unable to service their mortgages, and were forced to live in squatter camps. There was rioting as a result of food shortages. In November 1935 the Labour Party came to power and in January 1936 amended the Finance Act, which enabled the establishment of a State Housing Project. The first £10 million were provided at an interest rate of 1% per annum, while further advances in excess of this amount were charged at 1½% per annum. Within three years everyone was properly housed.

The Act also included a public works programme, which enabled the building of hospitals, schools, airports, dams etc. The unemployment rate declined by 75% to less than 7%.

---

48   Ibid., 2031.
49   Ibid., 2031.
50   Ibid., 2031.
51   Ibid., 2032.

Prime Minster of Canada, William Lyon Mackenzie King (1874-1950), warned that unless the issuance of currency was under the direct control of government, "all talk of sovereignty, of parliament, and of democracy, is idle and futile".

Senator Henderson referred to the benefits provided by Australia's state bank, the Commonwealth Bank of Australia (founded in 1912). He also revealed how the Australian government on the instructions of Sir Otto Niemeyer,[52] financial adviser to Montagu Norman, governor of the Bank of England, had been earlier forced "to reduce costs of government, balance governmental budgets and cut costs of private industry."[53] This austerity program had resulted in the Labour Party government being "slaughtered" by the "money powers,"[54] as it had not been "able to stand up to this octopus of big finance which has its grip on us, slowly throttling us."[55] His final comments were that "the quicker we realise that we are being bled daily for private profits [by commercial banks], the quicker we shall be rid of this incubus that hangs over our heads and prevents any real progress in the welfare of the community."[56]

In his concluding speech Senator Smith again referred to the newly created £200 million of fiduciary notes and said that "The sad and tragic part of it is that the system of which we are in the grip does not allow him [the Minister] to create that money as a monetary asset of the state, a new monetary asset of the State. It only permits him to bring it into existence as a debt owing by the state. It is common knowledge amongst

---

52 After 1924 Australia reverted back to orthodox finance by allowing private banks to create its money supply. By 1930 such were the financial difficulties of the Australian government that it could no longer even pay the interest on its overseas loans. Niemeyer was sent as the enforcer and claimed that Australia was "living beyond its means" and that it would have to "accept a lower standard of living." Former Prime Minister Billy Hughes (1915-23) correctly diagnosed what was at stake when he said that "We are 'hewers of wood and drawers of water' (Joshua 9:27). We are to produce materials for Britain's industry and – in order that Britain may be able to compete in the markets of the world, we must produce them cheaply – the cheaper the better." *Sir Otto Niemeyer's Report: Bond or Free – Reply* by W.M. Hughes, 1930, 5.

53 Ibid., 2035.

54 Ibid., 2035.

55 Ibid., 2035.

56 Ibid., 2036.

people who have the most fundamental knowledge of finance that the government spends money into existence and the banks lend it into existence. It goes through this process. The Minister passes out a bond of £1,000 and when the minister or the secretary or whoever it is has passed that bond, he has in fact created a new £1,000 and that is where the new money, the £200,000,000 that now exists, came from.[57]

Senator Smith then proceeded to give a favourable account of the state banking system in National Socialist Germany.

> "One of the most astonishing things which I think even the Minister himself will probably marvel at is the fact, that Hitler – I hope nobody is going to create a red herring if I mention Hitler because I am no supporter of Hitler – when he came into power he had £4,000,000 of gold in the Reichsbank, probably enough to carry on the war for six hours. We can all learn things from others, including Hitler. One of the most astonishing things to most of the orthodox financiers and economists of the world was that within a short space of time Germany was in full production. She was feeding and clothing and housing her people, and building up the greatest war machine the world has ever known. The orthodox financiers and economists said: 'Germany is bankrupt, how can she do it, she has not got any money to fight a war?' I would like to just tell you, Sir, what Hitler said about it. He said: 'We laugh at the time when our national economists held the view that the value of a currency is regulated by the gold and securities lying in the vaults of a State bank; more especially, we laugh at the theory that its value was guaranteed thereby. We have instead come to learn that the value of a currency lies in the productive capacity of a nation.'"[58]

---

57   Ibid., 2044.
58   Ibid.,2045-46.

He also cited an article in *The Times* of November 13, 1940, which said that "Germany adopted a new monetary policy after which Germany ceased to experience any financial difficulty. In this country [Great Britain] the people suffer the burden of heavy and increasing taxation, compulsory savings, or the issue of enormous public war loans. Quite the contrary [in Germany]. Recently, an important tax was abolished. Public savings bank deposits touch new monthly records again and again. Money is so plentiful that the interest rate on Reich loans could recently be reduced from 4½ per cent. to 4 per cent. Hitler seems to have discovered the secret of making something out of nothing."[59]

In his final remarks Senator Smith condemned the almost 300 years of control and power over the people, which the banks had exercised negatively, and deprecated the loss of an opportunity to create a prosperous and equitable society for all as follows:

> "The facts are these: that economic power, the central power, this greatest temporal power on earth which I have tried to describe to you, could not have remained and held its position for nearly three hundred years unless it had some very strong outer defences, without it having the means whereby it could retain and control that power, and in a so-called democratic system where people are led to vote for governments they like and vote against governments they dislike, the next line of defence which the money monopolists must have, is an organisation which can condition public opinion, condition the public mind. There is not one politician in this Senate who does not know that power."[60]

---

59   Ibid., 2047.
60   Ibid., 2051.

"Very well, Sir, we will have to have the political reasons when the Minister comes to review his department. I am very sorry, Sir, that the Minister has in my opinion lost the greatest opportunity that any minister has had in this country of ensuring that the dearest hopes of mankind, the dearest hopes of the soldiers, will be fulfilled, that is, that legislative instruments would be enacted by this Parliament to ensure that the days of unemployment were over, that the days of economic and social insecurity were over, convinced that these, the dearest hopes of the people, are to be betrayed. In the days of old, King Solomon built a temple to his god. Today the Treasury are building a legislative temple to their god, Mammon, and this is the instrument."[61]

The South African Reserve Bank Act was revised in 1989 at the instigation of the incumbent governor, Chris Stals. The only notable changes in the new Act were that Section 28 instituted a Gold and Foreign Exchange Contingency Reserve Account, Section 33 introduced a preservation of secrecy clause and Section 34 the sanctions pertaining thereto. The fact that such an important piece of legislation was not debated, but simply tacked on to a series of other bills of parliament for approval, is an indication of the decline in standards and ignorance about financial matters, which characterised the last years of white parliamentary rule.

In May 1948 there was much jubilation in many quarters when the National Party achieved "victory" at the polls. Instead of implementing a programme of monetary reform, they embarked on an unsuccessful program of social engineering, most of whose identified problems would have been resolved if the former course had been adopted.

---

61 Ibid., 2052.

Inside the South African Reserve Bank

In April 1994 having satiated themselves at the public trough, and after receipt of numerous and substantial financial inducements,[62] the so called "Nationalists" handed over the trappings, but not the real power itself to a new set of nomenklatura, whom the international bankers would be able more easily to control and manipulate. The new regime quickly introduced a number of illusionary and superficial changes, such as a new constitution, universal franchise and a change of symbols, but the underlying power base remained unchanged, as it has since 1652, in the hands of a clique of criminal bankers, who continue to exploit and enslave the people of South Africa.

---

62 The following conversation took place between former President PW Botha and President F W de Klerk when the latter visited Botha at his residence "Die Anker" in the Wilderness, southern Cape in 1994. The purpose of De Klerk's visit was to persuade Botha to appear before the Truth and Reconciliation Commission. Botha refused to entertain the idea.

Botha:	Wat van al daardie geld wat jy gevat het?
	What about all that money which you have taken?
De Klerk:	Meneer, ek het baie weggegee.
	Sir, I have given a lot away.
Botha:	Jy het ons weermag in die steek gelaat. Jy het ons land en ons mense verraai.
	You have let down our defence force. You have betrayed our country and our people.
De Klerk:	Meneer, jy beledig my nou, ek sal nou gaan.
	Sir, you insult me now, I shall now go.
Botha:	Ek roep eers my vrou dan kan jy dankie sê vir die tee wat sy jou bedien het.
	I will first call my wife then you can say thank you for the tea which she has served you.

As related by PW Botha to his second wife Barbara Botha. De Klerk is believed to have received initially upwards of R40 million in bribes, which at that time had a value of about $16 million, while according to a recent report in 2010, De Klerk had amassed an investment portfolio worth over one billion Swiss francs at EFG Bank von Ernst, Egertastrasse 10, Fl-9490, Vaduz, Liechtenstein. See also E. Rhoodie, *P.W. Botha, The Last Betrayal*, SA Politics, Melville, South Africa, 1989, 299 pp. and F.W. de Klerk, *Die laaste trek – 'n nuwe begin Die Outobiografie*, Human & Rousseau, Cape Town, 1998, 391-2. In the early 1990s Nelson Mandela is believed to have had £20 million on deposit with Barings Bank. For the Rothschilds, whose wealth has been estimated in the hundreds of trillions of dollars, control of South Africa was obtained for petty cash – money which they had already created out of thin air.

Chapter III

Director of South African Reserve Bank

That they (the Jews) took usury, though they were forbidden; and that they devoured men's substance wrongfully; we have prepared for those among them who reject faith a grievous punishment.
— The Holy Q'uran, Sura 4. 161.

Election as Non-Executive Director

I have been a shareholder in the South African Reserve Bank since 1986. The shares bought at 80 cents each yielded 12.5% per annum, which was a respectable return bearing in mind the high level at which interest rates were prevailing at that time. Over the following years it became apparent that both capital and income were continuing to decline in value, and as I was later to find out, it was largely the fault of the SARB for having delegated the right to create the nation's money supply to private banks at interest, which is the primary cause of inflation.

At the OGM held on August 27, 2002 I put forward a special resolution to amend the SARB Act, which would change the Bank's name to "South African Reserve Bank Limited" in order to reflect its true status as being that of a private bank and not a government controlled institution. Although only 38% of the shareholders voting supported the resolution, it indicated that there were a number of shareholders who were sufficiently interested in how the Bank was being run.

At the following year's OGM, held on August 23, 2003 a well motivated proposal was made by way of a special resolution to amend the Bank's Act to permit shareholders

Director of South African Reserve Bank

Tito Mboweni former Governor of the South African Reserve Bank.

to share in the profitability of the Bank as a means of compensation for the 99.5% loss in the purchasing power of the rand[1], which took place since the Bank commenced its operations on June 30, 1921. The 10% of profits allocated to the statutory reserve,[2] which at that time stood at R354,504,000, was identified as a possible source for funding an increased shareholder dividend. I also made myself available for election as a shareholders' representative on the Board of the Bank.

The response received from shareholders was very encouraging and included an endorsement from the South African Free Market Foundation. The Bank's reply that it was is not a "profit-driven" institution was a false contention, since as far back as 1944 Mr Albert Payne speaking in the

---

1   *South African Reserve Bank, History, functions and institutional structure,* 2011, 17.

2   The statutory reserve was created in 1921. The original intention was to build it up until it matched the share capital of £1 million. This occurred in March 1936.

House of Assembly debate on the SARB bill said that the bank is a "profit-making institution",[3] a statement which was not contradicted by anyone present then. If the Bank was not profit-driven, it would have been established as a non-profit making entity, such as a charity.

Prior to the 2002 OGM, the SARB had been very lax about the rules governing its meetings. Shareholder representatives, seven in number, were elected by a show of hands and it was never certain if all those hands raised were those of shareholders. For the first time in its history the Bank printed proper ballot papers.

My opponent for election as a shareholders' representative was sitting director Brian Gilbertson, the recently retired CEO of BHP Billiton, who was one of the Bank's more well-known board members. The results of the voting were that 70.3% of the shareholders approved the special resolution and 71.1% of votes were in favour of my election as a non-executive director.

The Bank was naturally concerned by the election of an outsider, which Mr Gilbertson believed could obtain considerable publicity both locally and overseas. The SARB's board commiserated with Mr Gilbertson on the loss of his seat and raised the possibility of his being appointed in the future as a government representative, of which there are now four. The Board issued a statement to the media containing three elements.

(i) The board's disappointment at the loss of Mr Gilbertson's experience and wisdom, (ii) the Board's opposition to the special resolution proposing an increased dividend, and (iii) the Board's concern about the private shareholding in the governance structure of the Bank.

---

3 House of Assembly Debates, May 3, 1944, 6449.

Director of South African Reserve Bank

There was something of a media flurry[4] for a day or two, which soon died down. One of the more balanced responses was written by the previous governor, Chris Stals, in an article in *Rapport* of September 21, 2003 headlined "*Reserwebank trots op eie bene*" (Reserve Bank proud of its achievements), in which he raised the prospect of the new director perhaps making a useful contribution to the management and policies of the Bank.

At my first board meeting on November 14, 2003, Governor Tito Mboweni barely shook my hand. However, as we got to know each other better, a more cordial relationship developed, which culminated in my attendance at the graduation ceremony held at the University of Stellenbosch on December 10, 2010, when he was awarded an honorary doctorate in economics.

Newly appointed directors have much to learn about how a central bank operates. To reduce that deficit in their knowledge, a two day induction course is organised which is spent on meeting the heads of departments and visiting the SA Mint, SA Bank Note Company and the SARB College. At meetings of the Non-Executive Directors' Committee, in-house speakers are invited to speak on various topics. However, it came as something of a surprise to realise that none of the non-executive board members had any understanding of how the fractional reserve banking system functions and how money is created. I did once make a proposal that this matter needed to be addressed, if board members were to play any meaningful role in assisting the bank in the execution of its macro-economic responsibilities. It was duly noted, but nothing came of it. In order to rectify this specific lack of

---

4   Beeld, August 28, 2003, *Business Day*, August 24 & 27, 2003, *Business Report*, August 27, 28 & 31 and September 4, 2003, *Cape Argus*, August 27, 2003, *Citizen*, September 2, 2003, *Financial Mail*, August 29, 2003, *Finance Week*, August 13, 2003, *Rapport*, August 31, 2003, *Sunday Argus*, September 9, 2003, *Sunday Independent*, August 31, 2003 and *Sunday Times*, August 31 and October 4, 2003.

knowledge I would submit articles at NEDCOM meetings concerning the problematic nature of the fractional reserve banking and other related matters. I also occasionally gave articles to Governor Gill Marcus to read. One of them concerned the remarkable performance of Belarus, which between 2000 and 2008 achieved an average growth rate of 9% per annum, principally because of its state banking system. Marcus always said that she would read them, but I never heard anything further and have to assume that either she did not read them or perhaps it was a case of her not having understood them.

In 2004 the Board was confronted with a rather delicate problem when in June the deputy governorship of Gill Marcus came up for renewal. She had previously worked for 20 years (1970-90) in London at the ANC's Department of Publicity and Information gathering statistics and, in between selling sandwiches at her father's shop, had also studied for a Bachelor of Commerce degree through a correspondence college. In 1994 when the ANC was elected, she was appointed Deputy Minister of Finance, while Mr Mboweni was appointed as Minister of Labour. In 1999 when Chris Stals retired as governor, she was resentful of the fact that Tito Mboweni was appointed ahead of her as governor of the SARB, believing that her superior knowledge of economics and experience in retailing entitled her to this appointment.

From about 2003 she devised a strategy to unseat Mr Mboweni from his position as governor. She started to compile a dossier listing alleged breaches of corporate governance, which in her opinion were taking place in the Bank. Furthermore she undertook a *sub rosa* investigation into the personal conduct of Mr Mboweni and, *inter alia*, would observe his consumption of alcohol at meals, visit the basement of the bank building to see if his car was parked there when he was not in his office and kept a

Director of South African Reserve Bank

record of his attendance at meetings. When Mr Mboweni found out what Ms Marcus had been conspiring to do, he was naturally incensed at her dishonorable and disloyal conduct. Clearly there existed sufficient grounds in law to have Marcus removed as deputy governor of the Bank, but in order to prevent a scandal, Mr Mboweni refrained from taking any action and broke off all social contact with her. I noticed that at board meetings Gill Marcus did not have much to say and that Mr Mboweni seemed to ignore her. At her last meeting on June 18, 2004 in Cape Town shortly before her contract expired, I recall her complaining bitterly to a few of us in the board room before lunch that she still did not know where she stood and in an emotional manner said that "He won't tell me anything." On June 30, 2004 a Bank official informed Gill Marcus that her services were no longer required and requested her to clear her desk and leave the Bank's premises. Thus there was no valedictory dinner with musicians in attendance and the presentation of a gift, as is customary when governors and deputy governors leave the Bank and she departed seemingly in disgrace. Finally, it may be noted that there is no letter of resignation in her personnel file.[5]

At the Board meeting held on November 12, 2004, the Board had to clear up the fallout left by Gill Marcus, which had resulted in the impugning and tarnishing of Mr Mboweni's integrity. Mr Mboweni recused himself. After her bogus report had been considered, it was unanimously rejected and Mr Mboweni was informed that he had the Board's full confidence. In December 2007 there was a change in leadership of the ANC at Polokwane (Pietersburg) and Mr Mboweni's backer President Thabo Mbeki was forced to resign. This resulted in Mr Mboweni not being reappointed by the Zuma regime in 2009.

---

5 C. Bisseker, *The Financial Mail,* August 20, 2004. A highly ironic interview in which Gill Marcus puts on a brave face about her dismissal from "the best job in the world."

On July 20, 2009 it was announced that Gill Marcus would be Tito Mboweni's replacement. There were naturally some internal misgivings about her appointment in view of the fact that she had left the Bank in 2004 under a cloud. At her first Board meeting on November 20, 2009 she introduced some curious changes. She announced that meetings would no longer be recorded and thus an accurate record of what had been said would no longer be retained. This situation would permit the airbrushing of minutes, which did in fact occur on a number of subsequent occasions. There was a breakdown in hierarchy and lack of formality brought about by the introduction of first name terms, the removal of name displays at board meetings, and the seating of senior non-executive directors next to the deputy governors was no longer mandatory. The listing of the names of directors in order of seniority was discontinued. There was also an insistence that board packs (the property of individual directors) be left behind for shredding – a rather inane requirement in view of the fact that a director could photocopy anything he or she required prior to the meeting.

She also announced that in future she would be adopting a recommendation of the King II Report on corporate governance which limits the term of office of non-executive directors to three terms of three years each. This resulted in the jettisoning of valuable skills acquired over many years. At the following year's annual board evaluation the five most senior non-executive directors (including myself) who had almost 50 years of experience between them and who co-incidentally had all served while Gill Marcus was deputy governor, were all asked to resign before the expiry of their terms – a request on the face of it ostensibly not unconnected with the fact that we were all aware of her dubious past.

In May 2010 legislation was put forward to amend the Act, ostensibly to prevent a German shareholder, Mr Michael

Dürr who with his family and friends had built up a holding of just over 10% or 200,000 shares in the capital of the Bank from becoming a non-executive director. In future only one family member of a group of so called "associates" would be entitled to vote on his or her maximum permitted holding of 10,000 shares. My understanding was that Mr Dürr, who is a proponent of monetary reform, had never had any intention of wanting to become a director, and that was what he had indicated when I first met him as part of a Bank delegation at his farm in Gansbaai on April 5, 2007. The source of Mr Dürr's dissatisfaction was the lack of corporate governance and the unsatisfactory way in which the Bank was being run. At the time of writing, he was planning to settle his dispute with the Bank in an international court of arbitration in terms of the Bilateral Investment Treaty between Germany and South Africa, which has been effective since April 4, 1998. In view of the fact that Germany is still under foreign occupation and is being governed under an illegal constitution,[6] viz., the so called Basic Law of 1949, which has no *de jure* recognition, theoretically South Africa possesses valid grounds to unilaterally annul this treaty. If such a scenario should eventuate the German government might well prefer to settle Mr Dürr's claims in an out-of-court settlement, rather than undergo a constitutional crisis. On two occasions I introduced written submissions advising the Bank to return to pre-1989 legislation where shareholders and dividends were correctly described as stockholders and interest respectively. This proposal would effectively have nullified Mr Dürr's campaign, but the advice was not heeded.

The amendment also provided for a panel headed by the governor, who would select candidates for the vacancies occurring among the seven shareholders' representatives.

---

6   S. Goodson, *Why the German Constitution is a Failure*, www.veteranstoday.com/2011/06/05-germany-still-under-the-control-of-foreign-powers

Shareholders would thus be denied the opportunity of electing a candidate of their own choice and who would moreover be able to speak on behalf of their interests. This authoritarian and undemocratic legislation, enables the governor to cherry pick his or her own type of candidate. The amendment also provided for the appointment of an additional non-executive director by government thereby altering the balance of the Board in favour of eight government appointed representatives as opposed to the seven elected shareholder representatives. This measure compromises the much vaunted "independence" of the Bank, which will be analysed in greater detail in Chapter V.

South African Bank Note Company Ltd

At the board meeting held on September 22, 2010 I first became aware of problems being experienced at the South African Bank Note Company, when we were informed that the managing director, Mr Musa Mbhele, had been suspended for unexplained reasons. Thereafter a steady flow of articles appeared in the media, such as one in *Business Report* of December 5, 2010, in which a number of damning allegations about impropriety and a collapse in production standards were reported by Dianne Hawker. These reports[7] continued throughout 2011 and it was unsettling that none of them were either rebutted or explained by the Bank's management to the non-executive members of the Board and that the Board was being kept deliberately in the dark.

At the annual board evaluation held on September 16, 2011, I complained to Gill Marcus about this lack of communication

---

7   D. Hawker, SA minting boss in hearing over 'dodgy notes', *Business Report*, November 17, 2010; J-M. Duddy, Namibia: BoN Sticks to Guns on South African Scandal, *The Namibian*, November 17, 2010; D. Hawker, Bank's dodgy money, *Business Report*, December 5, 2010; Open Letter to Ms Gill Marcus and Dr Xolile Guma, Justice for All Forum, February 7, 2011; D. Hawker, Now Reserve Bank blocks R10, R20 notes, *Weekend Argus*, March 3, 2011; S. Ngalwa, Marcus 'gave banknote job to friend', *Business Times*, July 30, 2011.

and said that I was tired of reading in the media about the failures of the South African Bank Note Company and that these symptoms were indicative of a possible cover-up. She took exception to my criticism and escalated this matter at the next board meeting on September 29, 2011, where I was admonished for having questioned the integrity of the Bank.

On November 17, 2011 at the Non-Executive Directors' Committee meeting I presented a memorandum entitled "Fiduciary Responsibility in Respect of the SA Bank Note Company". The memorandum included a brief overview of the recent corruption scandal at the Reserve Bank of Australia, where R450 million in bribes had been paid by RBA's 50% owned subsidiary Securency in order to obtain contracts for their polymer bank notes, (coated with a protective varnish), from foreign countries,[8] and where the managing director, Myles Curtis, a former deputy governor of the RBA, was facing a nine-year prison term at that time. I emphasised the risks that such criminal behaviour could hold in respect of the reputation of the SARB. A proposal that two directors visit the SABN in order to ascertain the facts on the ground was refused at the board meeting held on November 30, 2011.

Meanwhile I met the former managing director of the SABN, Musa Mbhele, on November 16, 2011 to see if he could shed any light on these disturbing allegations in the media. It transpired that in 2009 a syndicate headed by the head of security, Johan de Lange and his brother-in-law were responsible for stealing millions of rands of bank notes, and that the latter had an unauthorised safe in his office stuffed full of bank notes. Eventually the syndicate was exposed

---

8   Dirty Money: How the central pillar of Australia's financial system, the Reserve Bank, became ensnared in an international bribery scandal, *Australian Broadcasting Corporation*, Four Corners, Reporter: Nick McKenzie, May 24, 2010. See also Reserve still not off the hook on Securency, July 2, 2011, http://www.smh.com.au/business/reserve-still-not-off-the-hook-on-securency-2011070 20110701-1gv5p.html

after Roux and a colleague Joseph Maré were caught buying cycads with new bank notes at a Pretoria nursery.[9]

Mr Mbhele then asked the SABN board to appoint a team of forensic investigators in order to solve this problem. Gary Zulberg, apparently an "expert" in these matters, was appointed by Gill Marcus to lead the team. Not much is known about Gary Zulberg's expertise, except that he has been a close friend and confidant of Gill Marcus for a long time and during the "struggle years" had something to do with ANC finances. In the past he has provided advice for construction projects, and was once the manager of a steel factory. He does not appear to have any qualifications, as he frequently boasts that he does not even possess a standard six certificate.

Gary Zulberg forced himself into Mr Mbhele's office, despite the fact that he had been allocated an office of his own and soon started pushing him around and interfering with his duties and with affairs that did not concern him. On the morning of Friday, 18 June 2010 matters came to a head at the office of Mr Mbhele when he included in the Board's Audit and Risk documents, a statement that the project to install the new 3D Edward printing system, was going to be delayed due to Gary Zulberg's continual interference with steering committee meetings and his cancelling of important trips needed to view components of the 3DE system. These complaints were endorsed in writing by the Production and IT managers, Alec de Jongh and Chester Manuel respectively. Gary Zulberg then exploded. In the presence of Deputy Governor, Dr Renosi Mokate, and Messrs De Jongh and Manuel, he used abusive and foul language and said in a very threatening manner, "You will suffer for this!" Shortly thereafter on July 7, 2010 Mr Mbhele was placed

---

9   Confirmatory affidavit signed by M.V. Mbhele January 9, 2012.

on special leave, and although he obtained a court order, which reinstated him, Gill Marcus chose to illegally flout it and he was denied entry to the SABN. He was eventually dismissed six months later.

Crane Currency

At the beginning of 2010 there was a rumour that Crane Currency[10] of Tumba, Sweden might be invited to run the South African Bank Note Company. Of particular concern was what Mr Mbhele told me about a contract to import 80 million R100 bank notes from Crane. Mr Mbhele said that he had asked Gary Zulberg why bank notes were being printed in Sweden, as the local factory would stand idle according to the financial year production schedule. He replied that "the Swedes are friends of the Governor" and that the bank notes were being printed as a back-up. Apparently no contract was signed – at least at the offices of the SABN – and raw materials were diverted to Crane in May/June 2010. Crane experienced difficulties in printing the South African bank notes and requested secondment of a SABN engineer/technician to assist, but this was refused. At the Board meeting held on September 29, 2011 I asked Gill Marcus why the Board had not been informed about the Crane Currency order in view of the fact that the SARB had been printing its own bank notes since 1922 and why I had to read about it in the media. She replied that certain aspects of the SABN were "secret" and could not be disclosed to directors for "operational reasons."

According to Mr Mbhele, this order turned out to be a fiasco as the bank notes did not meet the required specifications. The bank notes were the wrong shade of blue, they lacked the ultra-violet security feature in the top left hand corner

---

10   Crane & Co. was founded in Boston, Massachusetts by Zenas Crane in 1801, although its first paper mill began producing bank note paper at Tumba, Sweden in 1753.

and had been cut to the wrong size measuring from 1 to 2 millimetres short. However, Gill Marcus decided that these defective notes should still be put into circulation. Complaints soon followed from commercial banks, supermarkets etc. and the Bank's reputation was seriously undermined. In April 2012 the serial numbers of these dud notes were inadvertently duplicated on 3.6 million locally produced R100 bank notes at a cost of 65 cents each. The dud notes had to be destroyed and the SABN incurred a loss of R2.34 million.[11]

I am unable to say if Gill Marcus received a "secret" commission on the purchase of the bank notes printed by Crane Currency, but it may be stated that it is a standard custom to do so, particularly where third world countries are involved. Crane Currency has, for example, printed bank notes for third world countries such as Malaysia and Tanzania. It may also be noted that in the past Sweden has had close links with the ANC. Reference has already been made to the Securency scandal, where commissions of up to 25% were paid (to the detriment of the country concerned which would ultimately be paying for them) as opposed to the "norm" of 5%. In Germany, Gesiecke & Devrient is the largest printer of euros in terms of volume of the 18 participating countries. However, when it comes to overseas orders, so as to keep their local accounts clean, they run a subsidiary in Dubai, United Arab Emirates for the payment of commission payments to their mainly third world clientele which includes South Africa.

Nelson Mandela Bank Notes

On February 11, 2012 Gill Marcus announced that there would be a new series of bank notes with the image of Nelson Mandela. At that time there was no justification or

---

11 Costly mistake with defective outsourced R100 notes by Sweden, SME (Small Medium Enterprise) *News Desk*, May 20, 2012.

need to produce a new series of bank notes, particularly in view of the stress the production of a new series would place on the SARB's loss-making balance sheet. The dominant factor for undertaking this expensive venture was clearly for party political propaganda purposes on behalf of the ANC. Once again the Board was not informed that Gill Marcus's Swedish friends, Crane Currency, would be responsible for the production of the R20, R50 and R200 bank notes for the now mandatory "operational reasons", and in all probability a rich source of unauthorised commission payments has flowed from this new order. The new bank notes came into circulation on November 2, 2012. On July, 7, 2013 it was revealed that the metal security thread near the centre of the note had not been correctly embedded and could easily be lifted, creating according to the Johannesburg *Sunday Times* a "counterfeiter's haven."

South African Mint

Besides providing South Africa with its coins, the South African Mint has built up a sizeable business producing gold and other commemorative coins and medallions. In April 2011 disaster struck when it transpired that one-ounce Krugerrand gold coins were being minted underweight of gold i.e. 5% less,[12] although the overall weight of each coin remained the same. Krugerrands have been produced by the SAM since 1967 and have a well-established reputation in the international market place with the one-ounce coin being the most popular gold coin in the world, but this reputation has been irrevocably tarnished by this unfortunate event. According to a report from Bullion Street dated April 16, 2012[13], the mint "didn't have enough gold" and that out of 1,500 coins minted, six were found to be underweight. The

---

12 www.coinweek.com/world-coins/south-african...2011-proof...underweight

13 www.bullionstreet.com/news/sa-mint-yet-to-clarify-underweight-krugerrands

Silver Doctors website, seems to have detected a more sinister motive and wrote in their newsletter of April 17, 2012 : "As such, it is likely safe to conclude that this was an intentional skimming operation by the Reserve Bank of South Africa rather than a production glitch. A national mint producing investment grade gold coins for several months with debased gold is not accidental. Period."[14] The lesson for gold investors is not to buy any Krugerrands post-2010.

After the underweight coins had been discovered, dealers were made to sign confidentiality agreements which prevented them from talking about the problematic coins. This is in line with the SARB's dishonest policy, under Gill Marcus, of covering up all blunders and mistakes in the hope that they will somehow vanish. Subsequently the managing director, Andile Mvinjelwa, and the general manager of numismatic coins, Tom Davel, were dismissed on May 31, 2012. Although the theft of half a million rands worth of R5 coins was mentioned at the Board meeting held on November 30, 2011, ten months later when I attended my last board meeting on February 23, 2012, the Board had still not been informed about the gold coin debacle, no doubt for the now customary "operational reasons."

Suspension

My efforts at trying to establish the truth did not endear me to the SARB's management, and on February 13, 2012 a special meeting was held where I was more or less forced to admit that I had erred. In my written reply I acceded to these demands, but reserved my constitutional right to interact with the media regarding non-banking matters. This was refused and at the Board meeting held on February 23, 2012 I was suspended. At the beginning of

---

14   www.silverdoctors.com/...underweight-krugerrands-were-produced-in-2011

Suspension

April 2012 I had to appear before a retired judge, Advocate John Myburgh, who would decide whether my suspension should be lifted or maintained.

I attended his chambers in Sandton, Johannesburg April 2-3, 2012. From the outset Mr Myburgh adopted an adversarial line of questioning and it soon became apparent that he was not in the least bit interested in my point of view and that in order to justify his substantial fee, I was to be the victim of a stitch-up. He was nonetheless clearly concerned when I told him that I was unable to trust Gill Marcus because of her unseemly behavior towards Tito Mboweni in 2003-04. That afternoon he scurried off to Pretoria, where under oath, Gill Marcus "readily accepted" that there had been "a breakdown in the relationship between her and Mr Mboweni", but denied that she had been "dismissed from the Bank."[15]

A few days later Mr Myburgh's farcical report arrived on my desk. One of his more amusing conclusions as to why I had breached my fiduciary duty to the Bank was that I did "not possess the knowledge and skill required of a Bank director."[16] I rejected his report in its entirety listing 20 objections. Myburgh's failure to interview important witnesses, such as Mr Mboweni and his abuse of the rules of evidence, constitute a serious breach of legal ethics and unprofessional conduct, which warrant an investigation by the Gauteng Law Society.

---

15   Ex parte South African Reserve Bank In re. S.M. Goodson, Draft Report, April 5, 2012, 60.
16   Ibid., 88.

Chapter IV

Reserve Bank's "Holocaust" Revisionist

"If our nation can issue a dollar bond, it can issue a dollar bill. The element that makes the bond good, makes the bill good... It is absurd to say that our country can issue 30 million dollars in bonds and not 30 million dollars in currency. Both are promises to pay, but one promise fattens the usurers and the other helps the people".[1]

— Thomas Edison

The lurid disclosure of my being a 'holocaust director' was plastered on newspaper billboards throughout Johannesburg and Pretoria on the morning of Friday, April 13, 2012 and was the main article in the business section of the *Mail & Guardian* weekly newspaper. My disclosure about Gill Marcus's attempted *coup d'etat* had clearly unsettled her and retaliation swiftly followed with an attempt to destroy my credibility and character by means of this subversive and libelous article, which she organised with the co-operation of a gullible reporter Lisa Steyn and her editor Nic Dawes.[2] When I asked Miss Steyn what the urgent and inexplicable reason was for her wanting to interview me, which interview I refused, she replied, "Because you are a director of the Reserve Bank!" The article, which alleged that I was a

---

1 The *New York Times*, December 6, 1921.
2 At a farewell banquet held in honour of John Swinton (1829-1901), Head of Editorial Staff of the *New York Times*, he said *inter alia* the following: "The business of the journalists is to destroy the truth; to lie outright; to pervert; to vilify; to fawn at the feet of mammon, and to sell his country and his race for his daily bread. We are tools and vassals of rich men behind the scenes. We are jumping jacks, they pull the strings and we dance. Our talents, our possibilities and our lives are all the property of other men. We are intellectual prostitutes." The article may be found at www.mg.co.za/article/2012-04-13-reserve-banks-holocaust-denier. For a rebuttal see K. Bolton, Reductio ad Hitlerum as a Social Evil, *Inconvenient History*, Vol. 5, No. 2, Summer 2013 http:// inconvenienthistory.com/archive/2013/volume-5/number-2/reduction-ad-hitlerum

Reserve Bank's "Holocaust" Revisionist

Holocaust Denier, had its desired effect, at least in certain circles, and became "hot" news on Jewish websites throughout the world. There were 98 responses to the article on the *Mail & Guardian's* website and the response from Adriaan du Toit probably sums up the inanity of it best - "Slow news day M&G? This article is a piece of sensationalist trash", while attorney Raymondt Dicks[3] identified the real purpose of the article – "This article reeks of a smear campaign. May we ask what the special relationship is between M&G and SARB. This we will never know because M&G has no morals when it comes to proper reporting as it writes its articles based on dictation and without proper investigation."

The following morning of April 14, 2012 a heated exchange took place at the farmers' market in Sedgefield, southern Cape known as "Wild Oats". Gill Marcus has a house in Knysna and this market, which sells mainly organically produced fruit and vegetables, is a popular venue for local and nearby residents. The following parley took place.

"Is your name Marcus?"
"Yes."
"My name is Barbara Botha, I was PW's wife.[4] Why did you place that article in the *Mail & Guardian*?"
"I didn't write it."
"Yes, but you knew all about it.
"No, I didn't."
"Yes, you did."
"No, I didn't."
"Yes, you did."

This altercation lasted for about five minutes, after which Gill Marcus retreated with her bodyguards visibly shaken and with guilt written all over her face.

---

[3] Mr Dicks is legal adviser to the New Economics Rights Alliance, which is challenging the legality of securitised home loans in the courts. See also www.newera.org.za

[4] P.W. Botha, one-time President of South Africa

The "Holocaust"[5]

On June 28, 2011 I participated in a radio programme of the Texas-based Republic Broadcasting Network[6] hosted by Deanna Spingola with the topic of discussion being "Is Germany's Constitution a Failure?" America is one of the few remaining countries in the world where freedom of speech is not only enshrined in law (the First Amendment of the US Constitution), but also practised, and I was informed that I could say whatever I wished. In the course of a two hour interview the question came up as to whether Germany is being exploited by being forced to pay reparations, currently in excess of $100 billion. I replied that the "Holocaust", in which I do not believe, was being used as an instrument to blackmail the Germans into having to pay vast sums in lieu of an event for which no documentary or forensic proof exists.

I have never denied the "Holocaust", as to this day I have been unable to establish what exactly occurred and have yet to read or see any evidence which has probative value. I have therefore adopted the status of a sceptic in the spirit of the Descartian maxim of *de omnibus dubitandum est* – everything has to be doubted, without which principle scientific progress and civilisation is impossible. In terms of the Aristotelian general principle of scientific enquiry, one must first seek the facts and then seek to explain them. In the absence of verifiable facts and the legal sanctions imposed by 16 European countries,[7] which

---

5   According to Rabbi Moshe Aryeh Friedman of New York "The Holocaust is a successful historical fiction", *Suddeutsche Zeitung*, December 12, 2006, 7. M.H. Glyn, *The American Hebrew, The Crucifixion of Jews Must Stop!*, October 31, 1919. The six million figure is of cabbalistic significance to some Jews and between June 11, 1900 and September 3, 1939 it appeared in at least 150 articles, books and periodicals with the claim that six million Jews were suffering or about to be killed. In this article by Glyn it is alleged that "Six million men and women are dying from lack of the necessaries of life" and that it is a "threatened holocaust."

6   RBN is one of the larger conservative American radio stations based in Texas and in December 2012 had 43 hosts.

7   As at April 2014 17 countries, which impose fines and /or prison sentences for denying the "Holocaust", are Austria, Belgium, Canada, Czech Republic,

prohibit any form of discussion of these so-called facts and which impose heavy fines and imprisonment of up to 20 years if one does so; one is compelled to assume that the "Holocaust" is not an historical fact. This becomes evident when it is realised that it may not be subject to any form of re-interpretation, reassessment and critical analysis, as is the custom with all other historical facts. The "Holocaust" narrative therefore possesses all the accoutrements of a dogma, which has been codified into a form of religion, and as Gilad Atzmon, the Israeli musician and author, has written in *The Wandering Who*,[8]

> "It could well be the most sinister religion known to man, for in the name of Jewish suffering, it issues licences to kill, to flatten, to nuke, to annihilate, to loot, to ethnically cleanse. It has made vengeance into an acceptable Western value."

Readers, who have an open mind and wish to view this matter in an objective manner, might like to consider the following rhetorical questions.

(i) Did International Jewry make a world-wide declaration of war on Germany without the slightest provocation, less than two months after the National Socialists were democratically elected? Yes. On March 24, 1933 such a declaration was made and was well publicised in the international media.[9] Germany was thus fully entitled to intern suspected Jewish trouble makers and to take whatever action was necessary in order to protect the sovereignty of the German state.

France, Germany, Greece, Hungary, Israel, Liechtenstein, Lithuania, Luxemburg, the Netherlands, Poland, Portugal, Romania, Slovakia and Switzerland.

8 H. Mahler, *Das Ende der Wanderschaft Gedanken über Gilad Atzmon und die Judenheit*, 2013, 63pp.

9 The headlines of the *The Daily Express*, Friday, March 24, 1933 read as follows: "Judea Declares War on Germany Jews Of All The World Unite In Action." The *New York Times* had the same Headlines. Ironically, a resolution at the World Zionist Congress held on September 5, 1933 calling for action against Hitler was defeated by 240 votes to 43.

March 24, 1933 - Declaration of war on Germany by International Jewry.

(ii) Was *Kristallnacht* (Night of Broken Glass) on November 9, 1938 a false flag operation staged by Jewish Zionists? Yes. In reaction to a British parliamentary proposal to guarantee Palestine to the Palestinians and to encourage Jewish emigration from Germany - preferably to Palestine - a German diplomat was murdered by a deranged Polish Jew, who had been set up by a French Jewish organisation known as the La Ligue Internationale Contre l'Antisemitisme. False telephone and telegram instructions were issued by *agents provocateurs* to *Kreisleiters* (district leaders) and other junior leaders to set alight Jewish businesses and synagogues. Unfortunately some of them did respond, and a large number of buildings were burnt down, and 89 people are alleged to have died. Hitler was furious when he heard about this outrage and ordered that it be stopped immediately.[10]

(iii) Does a written order issued by Hitler, Himmler, Göring, Heydrich or any other high ranking official to annihilate European Jewry exist? No.

---

10   I. Weckert, *Feuerzeichen: der "Reichskristallnacht", Anstifter und Brandstifter – Opfer und Nutzniesser*, Grabert Verlag, Tübingen, 1981, 301 pp.

The "Holocaust"

Photograph of British POWs football team at Auschwitz "death" camp 1944.

(iv) Are there any architectural drawings, technical plans, budgets, accounting documents etc. relating to the construction of homicidal gas chambers in existence, bearing in mind that the Allies seized over 3,000 tons of German documents? No.

(v) Are the eyewitness accounts reliable and consistent? No. As far back as January 1950 in an article written in *Jewish Social Studies*, the observation was made that "...most of the memoirs and reports [of Holocaust survivors] are full of preposterous verbosity, graphomanic exaggeration, dramatic effects, over-estimated self-inflation, dilettante philosophizing, would-be lyricism, unchecked rumors, bias, partisan attacks etc."[11]

More recently in August 1986, history professor and Dean of the Faculty of Arts and Science at the University of Caen, France, Michel de Bouaerd, who was a member of the French resistance and was interned in Mauthausen concentration camp, stated that "The documentation concerning the Holocaust is rotten, the documentation

---

11   S. Gringauz, *Jewish Social Studies*, New York, Vol. 12, 65.

about the system of the German concentration camps is permeated by a mass of invented stories, relentless repetitions of falsifications, especially in regard to numbers, and confusion and generalizations."[12]

(vi): Were all Jews deported from Germany to the camps? No, in the 1944 Berlin telephone directory dozens of Jewish organisations are listed, which indicates that a vibrant Jewish community still existed in the German capital at that time.

(vii) Was the official death toll at Auschwitz reduced (without explanation) from 4 million[13] to 1.1 million in 1991? Yes. After the forensic reports of Fred Leuchter,[14] an engineer, who has constructed homicidal gas chambers in the USA, and Germar Rudolf,[15] a researcher at the Max Planck Institute in Germany, were released, the Auschwitz museum authorities had no alternative, but to reduce the figure. *The Rudolf Report* (447 pages) has been peer reviewed by over 300 professors of inorganic chemistry in Europe. Not one of them could find a single mistake.

(viii) Is the real Auschwitz death toll substantially lower than 1.1. million? Yes. According to the complete Auschwitz records kept at the Russian Central Archives (Moscow No. 187603, microfilm 557-25, rolls 281-286,

---

12   *Ouest-France*, August 2-3, 1986, 6. (*Ouest-France* is France's largest circulating newspaper).

13   The 20 memorial plaques scattered around the complex, when the author visited it in 1976, and which were later removed in 1991, bore the following inscription: "Four million people suffered and died here at the hands of the Nazi murderers between the years 1940 and 1945."

14   F. Leuchter, *The Leuchter Report: The end of a myth, An engineering report on the alleged gas chambers at Auschwitz Birkenau and Majdanek, Poland*, David Clark, 1988, 132 pp.

15   G. Rudolf, *Dissecting the Holocaust: The Growing Critique of "Truth" and "Memory"* (Holocaust Handbooks Series 1), Theses & Dissertations Press, 2nd Revised edition, Chicago, Illinois, 2003, 616 pp.

The "Holocaust"

from May 1940 to December 1944) 103,424 persons died, of whom 98.4% perished from natural causes, principally typhus. Of the remaining 1,646, who were executed after due judicial process, 117 were Jews.

(ix) Do the messages between Auschwitz and Berlin decoded by Bletchley Park, England reveal any untoward events at that camp? No, nothing except for a spike in deaths from typhus during the summer of 1942.[16]

(x) Do the official accounts of World War II written by Winston Churchill, *The Second World War* (6 vols.), Charles de Gaulle, *Memoires de Guerre* (3 vols.), Harry S. Truman *Memoirs* (2 vols.), Dwight Eisenhower, *Crusade in Europe*, which contain 8,263 pages of text as well as introductory chapters, endnotes, appendices, indices etc., make any reference to "holocaust" or the murder of millions of Jews having taken place? No.

Auschwitz is the fulcrum[17] of the "Holocaust", but how was life experienced there in reality? The following list of facilities, some of which still exist, points to an entirely different purpose. There were playing fields, a volley ball court, a fencing club, a sauna, a post office at which there were twice weekly pick-ups and deliveries, (inmates were

---

16 http://www.whatreallyhappened.info/daily.html For an English translation of *Standort- und Kommandantur befehle des Konzentrationslagers Auschwitz1940-1945.* see http://altermedia-deutschland.info/pdf/ Englische_Uebersetzung%20_2000_Auszug_aus_Standort-_und_ Kommandanturbefehle_des_KZ_Auschwitz_1940-1945.pdf where all orders given at Auschwitz are documented, none of which indicates that anything of an irregular nature ever took place there.

17 In recent years the focus on the so called extermination camps has shifted from Auschwitz to Belzec, Majdanek, Sobibor and Treblinka, which are alleged to have been part of an operation known as *Operation Reinhardt*. In a monumental study, released in October 2013, C. Mattogno, J. Graf, T. Kues, *The "Extermination Camps" of "Aktion Reinhardt": An Analysis and refutation of factious Evidence", Deceptions and flawed argumentation of the "Holocaust controversies" Bloggers (Holocaust Handbook)*, Castle Hill Publishers, 2013, 1385 pp, the authors reveal that these camps were little more than transit facilities, and in the case of Bełżec also a labour camp.

Inside the South African Reserve Bank

allowed to send one postcard and one letter per week), a library with over 45,000 volumes, an office where inmates could lodge in private complaints with the commandant, halls for cinema shows and theatrical productions, 16 camp orchestras, a canteen, a photo laboratory, a camp university, classes offering courses in art and sculpture, an art museum, a designated building for religious services of all faiths, a brothel and a well equipped hospital with a maternity wing in which 3,000 babies were born, none of whom died.[18] Marriages were also permitted. There were regular visits by the International Red Cross, who would interview inmates in isolation, and nothing untoward was ever reported, including the existence of "gas chambers."[19]

---

18   Auschwitz a Photographic Tour compiled by Dr F. Töben, *The Barnes Review*, Washington D.C., Vol. XIII, No. 2, March/April 2007, 41-45.

19   An example of why scepticism of the "Holocaust" is justified may be found in Martin Gilbert's (real name Gibbertsohn) *Auschwitz and the Allies*, Arrow Books Limited, London, 1984 where on page 26 he writes that "The deliberate attempt to destroy systematically all of Europe's Jews was unsuspected in the spring and early summer of 1942: the very period during which it was at its most intense, and during which hundreds of thousands of Jews were being gassed every day at Belzec, Chelmno, Sobibor and Treblinka." By multiplying the 120 days of March, April, May and June by the minimum figure of 200,000 victims per day a total of 24 million is the result. In 1939 the American Jewish Committee of the Synagogue Council estimated the total Jewish population at 15.6 million, which by 1948 had advanced slightly to 15.7 million. Similar figures may be found in the *World Almanac of 1940* where on page 129 the Jewish population is recorded as being 15,193,359. The 1947 edition records on page 289 a figure of 15,690,000. See also Red Cross Report, *Documents sur l'activité du CICR en faveur des civils detenus dans les camps de concentration en Allemagne 1939-1945*, Geneva, published between 1948-1959, 3 vols., where there is no mention of the existence of "gas chambers".

In Public Record Office Document FO371/34551 dated August 27, 1943, Victor Cavendish-Bentinck, head of the British Psychological Warfare Executive admitted that there was not the slightest evidence that "gas chambers" existed and that such tales of their alleged existence were employed solely for propaganda purposes. In a hand written minute he wrote: "We have had a good run for our money with this gas chamber story we have been putting about, but don't we run the risk eventually we are going to be found out and when we are found out the collapse of that lie is going to bring the whole of our psychological warfare with it? So isn't it rather time now to let it drift off by itself and concentrate on other lines that we are running." See http://www.fpp.co.uk/Auschwitz/docs/Cavendish.html See also T. Christopherson, *Auschwitz – A Personal Account*, Sons of Liberty, 1979, 31 pp. W. Stäglich, a German judge, *The Auschwitz Myth*, Institute for Historical Review, 1986, 376 pp, and lastly on March 30, 1988 Joseph G. Burg, a son of a Romanian

The "Holocaust"

Jewish wedding in Westerbork 'Durchgangslager' Camp.

The swimming pool at Auschwitz, where Jewish Olympic swimmer, Alfred Nakache, practised regularly during the summer months.

On hot summer days children were served ice cream,[20] while a swimming pool with a diving board was available for use by both detainees and staff. One of the more famous users was a French Jew Alfred Nakache,[21] an Olympic swimmer, who practised regularly during the summer months. He was inducted into the International Jewish Sports Hall of Fame in 1993. Another well-known sportsman, who was allowed to continue his career as a heavyweight boxer while detained at Auschwitz, was Harry (Herschel) Haft.

Auschwitz was a giant labour camp providing a work force for the Buna-Werke factory of IG Farben, where artificial rubber was manufactured. It also functioned as an internment camp.

It should be noted that internment of enemy civilians is standard international practice. Thus in 1939 all German and Austrian nationals residing in the United Kingdom were sent to an internment camp on the Isle of Man, while in 1942 in the USA the entire Japanese population of 110,000 was sent to eight internment camps.

Slave labour was forbidden in Germany and all foreign workers were issued with an *arbeitsbuch* (work book) and received the same pay, insurance benefits and paid-up vacations as regular German workers.[22] When the camp

---

rabbi, who had visited Auschwitz in the latter half of 1945 and has written six books on World War II, testified under oath at the Ernst Zündel 'False News' trial in Toronto that the Holocaust was "a falsification of history" and that if this hoax was persisted with "there will never be a sincere relationship between the Jews and the Germans." http://ihr.org/books/Kulaszka/24burg.html.

20   Leaflet issued in 1985 by Ditlieb Felderer, author of *Anne Frank's Diary – A Hoax*, Institute for Historical Review, Torrance, California, 1979, 92pp. While researching for this book Felderer discovered that Anne Frank had a library card and made regular visits to the local library, which contradicts her alleged incarceration. Her parents were arrested because they had failed to report for duty at a labour camp in 1943.

21   Rivarol, No. 3014, 2009.

22   A typical example of this policy took place on August 7, 1944 when

The "Holocaust"

was abandoned on January 25, 1945, 80% of the inmates, rather than face the known brutality of the Soviet army, elected to travel west with the German camp guards. Most of the remaining 20% were either too elderly or too infirm to travel in the harsh winter conditions.

It needs to be stressed that nobody died as a result of starvation at Auschwitz and that the many harrowing scenes of emaciated and starving inmates found in camps like Belsen and Buchenwald were the direct consequence of the incessant Allied bombing and destruction of the German infrastructure, which prevented the transportation of food and medical supplies. From 1945 onwards many of the camps became overcrowded with the transfer of inmates from the east of the country which led to the spread of disease, and in particular typhus.

There is a commonly held belief that Hitler hated Jews, but there is no evidence supporting this contention.[23] He did of course severely criticize certain Jews, but criticism does not constitute hatred. Moreover, racial discrimination[24]

Amtsleiter Hans Biebow informed Jewish workers at a clothing factory in Łódź (Litzmannstadt), Poland that they would be transferred with their families and possessions (20kg each) west to a munitions factory, where they would be paid "in Reichsmarks" www.inconvenienthistory.com/archive/2013/volume_5/number_2/german_deportation_european_jews.php
In a post-war case, instituted by an ex-concentration camp prisoner (Jewish), who was suing in order to receive compensation for injuries he had received in an accident, while working in the camp during the war, a court official, Dr Florian Freund, who represented the Archives Department of the Austrian Resistance Movement, reported that the camp authorities did pay into social health care, accident and pension funds for all prisoners. Akten des Landesgerichtes für StrafsachenAz Wien (Archives of the Local Criminal Court): 26b Vr 7477/90; "Profil"–Wien_Nr. 24 vom 9.6.1997.

23 In *Hitler's Table Talk* compiled by M. Bormann, Ostara Publications, 2012, there are over 30 references, many of them detailed, to Jews. Although they are subjected to harsh criticism, there is not even a hint of an extermination programme.

24 The National Socialists' treatment of Black people was enlightened and humane when compared to the often brutal exploitation of American Negroes in chain gangs in the 1930s. The following example of official German policy is sourced from V.K. Clark, *Black Nazis!!! Minorities and Foreigners in Hitler's Armed Forces: An Unbiased History*, Create Space Independent Publishing Platform, 2, 238 pp. "15 Negroes and their families from previous German colonies are living in Germany. Most of them were soldiers fighting on Germany's behalf.

Inside the South African Reserve Bank

was not tolerated in the Third Reich. In the 1920s Hitler's trusted bodyguard and chauffeur, who saved his life on several occasions, was the Jew, Emil Maurice. Furthermore Hitler was not averse to appointing Jews to prominent positions in the Third Reich such as Dr Robert Ley (real name Levy), who headed the *Deutsche Arbeitsfront* (German Labour Front) and Dr Hjalmar Schacht (real name Hajum Schachtl), who was president of the Reichsbank (1933-39).[25] Over 150,000 Jews[26] of varying degrees of Jewish descent fought in the Wehrmacht, with many of them occupying the highest rank such as Field Marshal Erich von Manstein (née Lewinski).[27]

There were also dozens of full Jews serving voluntarily in the Gestapo and SS.[28] One of the more unlikely supporters

---

Most of them have no constant work and in the event that they do find work, their employer is subjected to hate campaigns and is forced to sack the Negroes again. I must point out that Negroes must have a possibility to earn a living, especially as most of them still have contact with their home country and will report about their circumstances in Germany. In co-ordination with the Foreign Minister it is important to select which Negroes should receive special protection and a work permit. However, it will still take some time before documentation has been issued. This information is confidential and should not be passed on as general knowledge, as some Party members will not accept and understand the reasons for the support of the Negroes. Only in areas where the Negroes live the district leaders should be informed that there are no objections for the employment of Negroes and no other action against individual Negroes is acceptable." Confidential circular no. 55/36 issued by Reichsleiter Martin Bormann. See also www.ww2f.com/topic/33711-hitlers-non-white-soldiers/

25 N. Mühlen, *Hitler's Magician: Schacht The Life and Loans of Dr Hjalmar Schacht*, trans., E.W. Dicks, George Routledge & Sons Ltd, London, 1938, 20 and 29.

26 B.M. Rigg, *Hitler's Jewish Soldiers: The Untold Story of Nazi Racial Laws and Men of Jewish Descent in the German Military*, (Modern War Studies), University Press of Kansas, Wichita, 2004, 504 pp.

27 There were in total 2 Field Marshals, 2 full Generals, 8 Lieutenant Generals, 5 Major Generals and 1 Admiral of Jewish descent. With a general commanding 100,000 troops, over a million German soldiers were under the command of Jews or part Jews. 20 officers of Jewish descent were awarded Germany's highest military decoration, the *Ritterkreuz des Eisernen Kreuzes* (Knight's Cross).

28 Prominent members of the Gestapo were the Jew Günter Abrahamsohn and the Jewess Stella Goldschlag. Jews also served as SS agents in organisations such as the Special Commando Wimmer. *Adelaide Institute Newsletter*, the Controversy of Black Nazis II, Ernest Young interviews Veronica Clark, December 17, 2013, No. 690, May 2013, 11. http://nspowerwolf.wordpress.com/2012/12/17/the-controversy-of-black-nazis-ii-an-interview-with-ernest-young/

The "Holocaust"

Generalfeldmarschall Erich von Manstein. Born Lewinski he was subsequently adopted by the von Mansteins. His Polish/Jewish antecedents did not hinder his career as a brilliant commander in the German Wehrmacht.

of Hitler was the *Lehi*,[29] a Jewish resistance group in Palestine, which later became known as the *Stern Gang* under the leadership of Yitzhak Shamir, Prime Minister of Israel (1983-84) and (1988-92). The men of the *Lehi* respected Hitler and persistently sought an alliance with Nazi Germany throughout 1940-41,[30] which included the offer of a battalion[31] of soldiers by Shamir.

The "Holocaust" has been ruthlessly exploited to gain financial largesse from other intimidated European countries and includes a shakedown of Swiss banks,[32] which were blackmailed in August 1998 into handing over $1.25 billion or face closure of their branches in the United States. German companies and more recently French national railroad SNCF have also been sued for unspecified amounts. So far 4.3 million Jewish "survivors" have claimed *wiedergutmachung* or compensation, even though the number of Jews living in countries occupied by Germany during World War II did not exceed 2.9 million.[33] Substantial portions of these compensation payments intended for so called "survivors" often do not reach them, but are embezzled by intermediaries, while more recently there have been a number of cases involving claims, which have been submitted by fraudulent "survivors".[34] The best known exposer of the "Holocaust" scam is Professor Norman Finkelstein, formerly of De Paul University, Chicago, whose parents apparently survived several years

---

29 *Lohamei Herut Israel* (Fighters for the Freedom of Israel).

30 www.ww2incolor.com/forum/archive/index.php./t-7724.html

31 A battalion can consist of between 230 to 1,200 soldiers with the most common number 1,000.

32 The official website of the Swiss Banks Settlement: In re Holocaust Victim Assets Litigation is www.swissbankclaims.com/overview.aspx

33 W. N. Sanning, *The Dissolution of Eastern European Jewry*, Institute for Historical Review, Torrance, California, 1983, 14.

34 Charges filed in $42.5 million fraud of Holocaust survivors, *Jerusalem Post*, September 10, 2010. The final figure in this fraud, which started in 1993, was $57 million. See P. Berger, How $57 Million Holocaust Fraud Unfolded at Claims Conference, *The Jewish Daily Forward*, May 9, 2013.

The "Holocaust"

Jewish Orchestra performing at Theresienstadt 'Konzentrationslager' Camp.
Photo taken by Kurt Gerron, Jewish wartime film producer.

Photograph of Jewish children in Theresienstadt taken by Dr. Maurice
Rössel, during an inspection by the International Red Cross, 1944.

at Auschwitz unscathed. In his landmark treatise *The Holocaust Industry: Reflections on the Exploitation of Jewish Suffering*, which has sold over half a million copies,[35] the financial aspects of this extortion racket are fully exposed.

Since December 27, 2009 the Jewish "Holocaust" and its mythical "gas chambers" have ceased to exist, at least in the mind of Professor Robert van Pelt. In the words of French Professor Robert Faurisson,[36] the doyen of historical revisionism: "Van Pelt is a Jewish researcher who, giving up the fight, has come to acknowledge that there exists at Auschwitz, capital of "the Holocaust", no evidence of an extermination of the Jews but only 'testimonies' *(sic)*. He recommends that the entire site of Auschwitz and Birkenau be surrendered to nature. In other words, if I understand correctly, the tens of millions of tourists or pilgrims who have visited the place have been and continue to be fooled with an abundance of false evidence. For me, the exploiters of the Auschwitz myth are not just making fools of the living but are also mocking the dead, whose real sufferings are thus relegated to make way for phantasmagorical tales born of sick brains and turned to profit by swindlers."[37]

For those Jews who are offended by billions of people who are unaware of or refuse to believe in their "Holocaust" religion, they do have the option to avoid such offence by emigrating to a country where such a belief is tolerated, viz. their national homeland Birobidjan. Founded in 1928 by Soviet leader Josef Stalin, it is similar in size to Switzerland and nearly double the size of Palestine, situated in an underpopulated and fertile corner of south east Russia. There are currently 75,000 inhabitants of this *oblast* or region, it has its own flag and the official language is Yiddish. The official

---

35   N.G. Finkelstein, *Verso*, New York, 2003, 256 pp.
36   Robert Faurisson (1929-) is a former professor of French literature at the University of Lyon, who has written extensively on the "Holocaust" from a revisionist point of view.
37   *Smith's Report* No. 194, November 2012, 9-10.

policy of the government of the Russian Federation is to move "toward its own final solution of the Jewish question, through voluntary resettlement of those members of the Jewish minority who refuse to integrate into Russian society and adopt Western culture".[38]

In a subsequent *Mail & Guardian* article[39] the author was slated for having "extremist views", and as one who admired the economic policies implemented by Adolf Hitler in National Socialist Germany. However, *au contraire*, this was the general view held at that time, as the following small sample of quotations from prominent persons attest.

David Lloyd George Prime Minister of Great Britain (1916-22):

"Yes, Heil Hitler. I say this because he is truly a Big Man... For the first time since the war, a general feeling of security and peace has prevailed. People are happier. Across the country, you meet a happy, fun-loving people. It is a much happier Germany I observed everywhere. And English, who I met on my trip through Germany, who are familiar with the country and people were impressed by these major changes. This wonderful phenomenon has been created by a single man... You can thank God you have such a wonderful man as your leader!"[40]

William Lyon Mackenzie King Prime Minister of Canada (1921-1930, 1935-1948) wrote in his diary on June 29, 1937:

"My sizing up of the man [Hitler] as I sat and talked with him was that he is really one who truly loves his fellow-

---

38 W. A. White, Vladimir Putin Still Pursuing Plan to Resettle Russia's Jews, *The Barnes Review*, Vol. XX, No. 3, May/June 2014, 29.
39 L. Steyn, *Mail & Guardian Business*, Shareholders give Gill Marcus a thumbs up, August 3, 2012, 2.
40 *The Daily Express*, September 17, 1936.

man, and his country, and would make any sacrifice for the good. He is a man of deep sincerity and a genuine patriot. As I talked with him, I could not but think of Joan of Arc. The world will yet come to see a very great man. He is distinctly a mystic."[41]

Winston Churchill Prime Minister of Great Britain (1940-45) and (1951-55) wrote in September 1937:

"In fifteen years that have followed this resolve, he has succeeded in restoring Germany to the most powerful position in Europe, and not only has he restored the position of his country, but he has even, to a very great extent reversed the results of the Great War ...whatever else might be thought about these exploits they are certainly amongst the most remarkable in the whole history of the world. If our country were defeated I should hope we should find a champion as indomitable to restore our courage and lead us back to our place among the nations."[42]

Houston Stewart Chamberlain philosopher:

"At one stroke you have transformed the state of my soul. That Germany in the greatest hour of its need can produce a Hitler testifies to its vitality."

Carl Gustav Jung psychologist:

"Hitler is a spiritual vessel, a demi-divinity; better still a myth."[43]

---

41 www.collectionscanada.gc.ca/king/023011-1070.05-e.html

42 Winston Churchill, *Step By Step 1936-1939*, Odhams Press, London, 1948. First published in *The Evening Standard*, September 17, 1935 and later repeated in *The Strand Magazine*, November 1935. This was six months before Churchill fell into the clutches of the moneylenders, where after his attitude towards Germany changed to the negative irrevocably.

43 N. Goodrick-Clarke, *Black Sun: Aryan Cults, Esoteric Nazism and the*

The "Holocaust"

Professor John Kenneth Galbraith (1908-2006) confirmed that by the late 1930s National Socialist Germany had achieved full employment at stable prices and that "it was in the industrial world an absolutely unique achievement".

HRH the Duke of Windsor:

"I have travelled the world and my upbringing has made me familiar with the great achievements of mankind, but that which I have seen in Germany had hitherto believed to be impossible. It is a miracle. One can only begin to understand it when one realises that behind it all is one man and one will – Adolf Hitler."[44]

James Kenneth Galbraith, Professor of Economics, University of Harvard:

"The elimination of unemployment in Germany during the Great Depression without inflation – and with initial reliance on essential civilian activities – was a signal accomplishment." "Germany, by the late thirties, had full employment at stable prices. It was in the industrial world, an absolutely unique achievement."[45]

President John F. Kennedy wrote in his diary on August 1, 1945:

"After visiting these two places (Berchtesgaden and the Eagle's lair on Obersalzberg) you can easily see how that within a few years Hitler will emerge from the hatred that surrounds him now as one of the most significant figures who ever lived. He had boundless ambition for his country, which rendered him a menace to the peace of the world, but he had a mystery about him in the way that he lived and in the manner of his death that will live and grow after him. He had in him the stuff of which legends are made."[46]

Politics of Identity, New York, New York University Press, 2002, 178.
44 *New York Times*, October 18, 1937, 12.
45 J.K. Galbraith, *The Age of Uncertainty*, Houghton Mifflin, Boston, 1977, 214.
46 J. F. Kennedy and H. K. Sidey, *Prelude to Leadership – The Post-War*

John Pierpont Morgan (1837-1913) was a Rothschild front man, who created the conditions for the founding of the US Federal Reserve Bank by instigating the Panic of 1907. He also provided the venue for the formation of this central bank at his Jekyll Island Hunt Club in November 1910.

Resignation

I was summoned to appear at another special meeting to be held on May 17, 2012 to discuss the Myburgh Report and my "fate." By then I had had more than enough of the Bank's antics and machinations and requested an exit strategy, which entailed compensation for all the meetings I would have attended if I had been a board member until July 27, 2012, the date on which my directorship would have terminated. I was forced to sign an agreement that I would not make any disclosures about the Bank or any of its officials in perpetuity. Disregarding the obvious undertones of blackmail and the Bank's complicity in the assassination of my character, such an undertaking is clearly *contra bonos mores*, and cannot therefore include any disclosures where malfeasance has occurred, particularly where such malfeasance is harmful to the public interest. In this regard it may also be noted that the public interest in the affairs of the SARB not only extends to how the implementation of monetary policy affects its welfare, but to the fact that 90% of the profits of the Bank, when it is profitable, have to be paid over to government. Thus any misappropriation of the Bank's funds, including those held by its subsidiaries, by an employee of the Bank, has a direct bearing on the public interest.

A few weeks later on May 23, 2012 I received a very menacing letter from the legal counsel of the Bank threatening me with criminal court action on the grounds that I had disclosed the contents of the Myburgh Report to Michael Dürr, the dissident shareholder. In view of the fact that I had not heard from him for many months this came as a complete surprise. After e-mailing him, it turned out that he had sent an e-mail to Gill Marcus dated May 10, 2012, which had said among other matters: "I understand that you were distracted by the meetings regarding the

---

Diary of John F. Kennedy, Regnery Publishing, Washington DC, 1995, 210pp.

Resignation

Goodson issue and his final removal." Well, presumably certain meetings were held regarding my removal and that is exactly what everyone that I spoke to said after Gill Marcus had arranged for the placement of that defamatory article in the *Mail & Guardian*.

From all the above events it can be seen that Gill Marcus is not a fit and proper person to be governor of the SARB. She should not have been appointed in the first place and is a typical example of an ANC cadre deployment. For the following reasons there exist sufficient grounds in law to have Marcus removed as governor of the Bank.

(i) She illegally attempted to unseat Governor Tito Mboweni.

(ii) She committed perjury by lying[47] under oath to Advocate Myburgh about her dismissal as deputy governor.

(iii) She deliberately orchestrated the libeling of a fellow director.

(iv) During each year of her tenure as governor the Bank has incurred losses amounting to R7.2 billion.

(v) She contravened the SARB Act.

(vi) She mismanaged the subsidiaries of the SARB.

(vii) She failed to provide any guidance in resolving the economic crisis.

(viii) She is not a person of tested banking experience and has no knowledge of alternative banking systems.

---

47 According to the Talmud "Jews may lie to non-Jews, Jews may use lies to circumvent a Gentile", *Baba Kamma* 113a; "Jews may swear falsely by use of subterfuge wording", *Schabouth Hag.* 6b and "Jews must always try to deceive Christians," *Zohar* 1160a. The instruction used is called a *mitzvot* (commandment) and bestows on the perpetrator a *berakhah* (blessing).

Chapter V

Defective Policies and Failures of the South African Reserve Bank

Whoever eats up, robs and steals the nourishment of another, that man commits a great murder (so far as in him lies) as he who starves a man or utterly undoes him. Such does a usurer, and sits the while on his stool, when he ought rather to be hanging on the gallows.
  - Martin Luther as quoted in *Das Kapital* by Karl Marx

Fit And Proper Directors

It has already been established in the previous chapter that Gill Marcus is not a fit and proper person to be governor of the SARB, but there have been other dubious appointments in the past.

On May 23, 2010 Mr Aboobaker Ismail, head of the Currency and Protection Services Department, was appointed a director of the SA Bank Note Company. According to testimony he gave at the Truth and Reconciliation Commission in May 1998, he was responsible for the explosion of 40kg of explosives in a car parked in front of the South African Air Force Headquarters building in Church Street, Pretoria on May 20, 1983, which resulted in the deaths of 19 and the injury of more than 200 people. He said that the building had been "an overwhelmingly military target."[1] Of the 19 dead, seven were female clerical staff belonging to the SAAF. If Mr Ismail had blown up a military barracks or installation at Voortrekkerhoogte army base, his organisation Umkhonto we Sizwe might have earned some credibility. Instead he

---

1   South African Press Association, Pretoria, May 6, 1998.

picked on mainly innocent civilians, both white and black, in a cowardly attack. In the event his pointless "struggle" had zero effect, as "power" was merely transferred from one set of puppets to another, and the enslavement of the South African people by the bankers continues unabated. As Johann Wolfgang von Goethe wrote in *Elective Affinities*, "None are more hopelessly enslaved, than those who falsely believe they are free."[2]

Another director, who does not appear to be fit and proper, is Mr Gary Ralfe, a former managing director of De Beers Consolidated Mines, who was elected as a shareholders' representative on June 30, 2011. At the same time as his election, a report in the monthly periodical *Muslim Views* revealed the findings of the London firm of lawyers, Slaughter and May, who had conducted an investigation into corruption at the De Beers Botswana mine. According to a 2012 survey undertaken by the US publisher of *Vault Magazine*, Slaughter and May is the most prestigious law firm in Europe. The report alleges that Louis Nchindo, former CEO of Debswana, whose headless body was found in the Kalahari bushveld on February 11, 2010, "and seven other De Beers nominees on the Debswana board, among them Nicky Oppenheimer[3] and Gary Ralfe, lined their pockets at the expense of the Botswana government by pushing up production at Debswana mines even when the price of diamonds was going down."[4] At a Special Board meeting held on February 13, 2012, Gary Ralfe had much to say for himself, including that I had been "underhand" in my enquiries into corruption at the SABN. Indeed.

---

2   *Die Wahlverwandtschaften*, 1809.
3   *Muslim Views*, June 2011, 3.
4   By a coincidence Nicky Oppenheimer was the fag (a schoolboy forced to do menial tasks) of Myron Kok at Harrow School, London in 1951. Kok has written a review of the companion volume, *A History of Central Banking and the Enslavement of Mankind*, Black House Publishing, London, 2014, 214 pp.

Previous Scandals

In May 1971 the Minister of Finance, Dr Nico Diederichs, a freemason and later CIA agent,[5] attended a meeting of the Bilderbergers on the island of Bermuda, without the knowledge of the South African government. He had been invited by one of the leaders of this secret organisation, David Rockefeller. One of its aims is to promote a New World Order and a single world government and central bank. There he met certain Swiss businessmen and came to an agreement whereby he would earn a commission on all South African government transactions with the Union Bank of Switzerland, as well as a commission on all gold sales transacted through Zürich. Bank accounts were opened in his name as well as a secret one for his commission payments. Although these acts were in contravention of the existing exchange control regulations, they were condoned by the governor of the SARB, Dr Theunis de Jongh.

In March 1976 Dr Robert Smit, a former employee of the SARB and South African representative at the IMF, discovered that large sums of foreign exchange were illicitly flowing out of the country with the co-operation of the SARB. When he approached the Minister of Finance, Senator Owen Horwood, another freemason, the latter said that he knew nothing about it. In September 1977, Dr Smit produced a report on the matter for the minister, in which he found after a visit to Zürich, that Diederichs had accumulated $17 million in his private bank account – an enormous sum at that time.[6]

Diederichs, who was then State President, faced imminent exposure and asked his CIA handler for assistance. A hitman

---

5 P.J. Pretorius, *Volksverraad, Die Geskiedenis agter die Geskiedenis*, Libanon-Uitgewers, Mosselbaai, Western Cape, South Africa, 1996, 181.

6 $17 million, after allowing for inflation, was worth $115 million or R1.15 billion at an exchange rate of $1=R10 in November 2013.

Previous Scandals

```
2)
COMMODITY:        GOLD BULLION
QUALITY:          50 M/T IN DORE FORM
FINESSES:         LIKE SPECIFICATION
DELIVERY:         KLOTEN/SWITZERLAND
PRICE:            LONDON SECOND FIXING
DISCOUNT:         2,5% (TWO,FIVE PERCENT)


PROCEDURE FOR BOTH TRANSACTIONS:
--------------------------------
MEETING IN LUGANO/SWITZERLAND IN INDOSUEZ BANK
EVIDENCE OF PRODUCT ---
                       --SIMULTANEOUSLY
EVIDENCE OF FUNDS   ---
CLOSING OF TRANSACTION IN ONE SO.
```

Delivery note for 50 tons of stolen South African gold.

"MacDougall" and a driver were provided. On the night of November 22, 1977 Jean-Cora and Robert Smit were separately murdered at their home in Selcourt, Springs, in the presence of Diederichs. Later the police examined the attaché case of Smit from which the incriminating report on the foreign exchange fraud had been looted by Diederichs. The Springs Criminal Investigation Department found Diederichs's finger prints on the case, but the matter was not taken forward.[7]

---

7   P.J. Pretorius, op.cit., 227-229. According to Advocate Pretorius a portion of this information was obtained from Mrs Emmarentia Liebenberg, a friend of Diederichs to whom he made a death bed confession.

Inside the South African Reserve Bank

During the last 15 years of National Party rule vast amounts of foreign exchange, with the connivance of the SARB, were stolen or misappropriated. Known as Project Hammer, 3,000 tons of South Africa's strategic gold reserve held mainly at Kloten Airport, Zürich, Switzerland were part of this gigantic heist. A portion of this stolen gold was used in 1989 to help bail-out struggling, too big to fail banks in the United States, and in particular Citibank, which were all facing insolvency. According to a document marked "Top Secret" MZ/HRB/10-10/98ser.Noj/IBI, provided in October 1998 by a German intelligence operator to Gerhard Laubsher of the South African Intelligence Agency citing the disappearance of $223,104,000,008 worth of South African gold, the following list of former employees of the South African Reserve Bank played a prominent role in this sordid affair.

James Cross	General Manager, Gold and Foreign Exchange
Barend Groenewald	Deputy Governor
Japie Jacobs	Deputy Governor
Jan Lombard	Deputy Governor
Chris Stals	Governor
Chris Swanepoel	General Manager/Secretary, Finance, Personnel and Secretariat
Christo Wiese	General Manger, Bank Supervision

This report which forms part of the Project Hammer file[8] also states that 50 tons of every 550 tons of gold produced annually at that time was stolen.

The CIEX[9] Report produced in 1999 by a privately-owned London firm of private investigators stated that they were

---

8   http://www.deepblacklies.co.uk/hammer_blurb.htm
9   Council for Investment, Export and Foreign Exchange and the Diaspora.

initially offered a recovery fee by government of 10% on the first R100 million and thereafter 7.5% on the balance recovered. The total sum misappropriated is in the region of R2.25 trillion. Included in this sum is R14 billion, which partly relates to the "lifeboat" fraud, whereby Bankorp, a bankrupt subsidiary of ABSA bank, was granted in 1985 soft loans at 1% per annum, which were then re-lent at 18%+ per annum.

In an article in *Noseweek* of September 2010, the authors raised the question as to why the SARB and the South African government decided "not to recover billions of rands, already set aside by ABSA bank for repayment."[10] To the observant reader it must now be obvious that the South African Reserve Bank, as well as all central banks throughout the world, are the implacable enemies of the people, and that their principal purpose is to serve the interests of private bankers.

Continuous Linked Settlement System

In 2002 the Continuous Linked Settlement System[11] was established with 39 settlement members and seven currencies. The alleged purpose of this system is to mitigate fluctuations in foreign exchange settlement rates. Currently the system covers 17 currencies. It has 74 shareholders, which are all banks, 63 members and over 9,000 active third party participants. The CLS settles about $5 trillion every day.

In December 2004 Deputy Governor Ian Plenderleith, who had been seconded by the Bank of England for a three year term to the SARB, organised South Africa's membership of this system. As a result of its membership, South Africa, along with all the other participating countries, has forfeited its own sovereign rights to control over its foreign exchange

---

10   *Noseweek*, September 2010, 13.
11   www.cls-group.com

holdings to a British and Swiss company, which is owned by over 80 commercial banks. This company is in turn regulated by the US Federal Reserve Bank of New York as an Edge Corporation.[12]

JP Morgan Chase & Co.

JP Morgan and Company acquired their name after Drexel, Morgan & Co. were renamed in 1895. JP Morgan has been subject to numerous mergers and demergers and was set up to house the American banking interests of the Rothschild family. It is the largest bank in the United States by assets, believed to be in the region of $2 trillion. The bank has been involved in numerous scandals, conflicts of interest and controversies since its inception, particularly in the last decade. In December 2002 JP Morgan paid $80 million in fines for having deceived investors with biased research.[13]

In 2001 JP Morgan paid $2 billion in fines for its role in financing the collapsed Enron Corporation, in 2002 $160 million in fines was paid to the Securities and Exchange Commission and in 2005 $2.2 billion was paid to the investors of Enron who had been defrauded.[14] In November 2009 JP Morgan paid $722 million in fines to the SEC after having sold fraudulent derivatives to Jefferson County, Alabama and charged higher rates of interest to offset bribes paid to county officials.[15]

---

12 An Edge Act Corporation, first implemented in 1919, is a banking institution with a special charter from the US Federal Reserve Bank, which permits it to conduct international banking operations and certain other forms of business without complying with state-by-state banking laws. In 1984 the Edge Act was expanded so as to allow companies engaged in international business, such as trading and shipping firms and international airlines, to provide full banking services, including taking deposits and granting loans.

13 en.wikipedia.org/wiki/JPMorgan_ Chase Controversies: Conflicts of interest on investment research.

14 Ibid., Controversies: Enron.

15 Ibid., Controversies: Jefferson County, Alabama.

JP Morgan Chase & Co

In June 2010 the United Kingdom Financial Services Authority fined JP Morgan a record £33.32 million for having failed to segregate client funds and corporate funds into separate accounts.[16] In January 2011 JPM paid $27 million in compensation to mortgagors who were serving in the US military, after having illegally charged higher rates of interest and in 18 cases having illegally foreclosed on properties.[17]

On December 20, Linette Lopez wrote in *Business Insider* that New York Attorney General Eric Schneiderman had ruled that any private entity can press securities fraud charges against JP Morgan Chase.[18] In May 2012 JP Morgan reported a $2 billion trading loss as a result of a series of trades in complex synthetic credit derivatives having gone wrong. Described as legal hedging at the time it was more likely to have been speculation. CEO Jamie Dimon said that it was "a terrible egregious mistake."[19]

On May 13, 2012 intelligence expert, Tom Heneghan reported that as a result of these losses JP Morgan faced financial decapitation.[20]

On May 15, 2012 the US Justice Department and the Federal Bureau of Investigation in New York announced that there would be a criminal probe into these losses. On May 14, 2012 it was reported that Sheila Bair, head of the Office of the Comptroller of the US Currency, had uncovered that JP

---

16 Ibid., Controversies: Failure to comply with client money rules in United Kingdom.

17 Ibid., Controversies: Mortgage overcharge of active military personnel.

18 L. Lopez, *Business Insider*, According To The New York State Supreme Court, Anyone Can Sue JP Morgan For Securities-Fraud www.businessinsider.com/new-york-state-supreme-court-rules-again

19 Washington's Blog, The Truth About JP Morgan's $2 billion loss, Global Research, May 16, 2012 www.globalreserach.ca/index.php?context=va&aid=30859

20 T. Heneghan, JP Morgan Fraud is CFTC (Commodity Futures Trading Commission) Fraud, May 14, 2012.

Morgan had violated the ratio distribution margin requirement of the Chicago Mercantile Exchange (CME) Group by writing naked cross-collateralised interest rate and foreign currency derivatives on the London LIFFE Exchange[21] at a 90% market ratio, when the CME Group required collateral of at least 50% of collateralised real assets to make the credit default trades between the two exchanges legal.

On June 5, 2012 former Assistant Secretary of the US Treasury, Dr Paul Craig Roberts wrote that JP Morgan was manipulating the silver market, which manipulation may eventually have disastrous consequences for the bank. "Morgan is the custodian of the largest long silver fund while being the largest short-seller of silver. Whenever the silver fund adds to its bullion holdings, JP Morgan shorts an equal amount. The short selling offsets the rise in prices that would result from the increase in demand for silver."[22]

On July 17, 2012 it was revealed that JP Morgan's loss had increased from $2 billion to $5.8 billion and that it had deliberately falsified its first quarter report filed with the SEC in order "to conceal its massive gambling losses." Other scandals highlighted were an investigation into manipulation of the London Interbank Offered Rate (LIBOR); advice given to clients to sell their JP Morgan mutual funds "when it was against the clients' interest"; a court case in which JP Morgan was sued by the US Federal Energy Regulatory Commission for alleged price gouging in electrical power markets by one of the bank's subsidiaries in California and the Midwest, and the announcement of a proposal together with other major banks and Visa and MasterCard "to settle allegations that they colluded to fix fees on credit card transactions, ripping off billions of

---

21 London International Financial Futures and Options Exchange.
22 P.C. Roberts, Financial Collapse At Hand: When is "Sooner or Later?", Global Research, June 5, 2012 www.globalresearch.ca/index.php?context=v&aid=31272

dollars from retailers and customers and violating anti-trust laws."[23] On October 1, 2012 Linette Lopez wrote in *Business Insider* that New York Attorney-General Eric Schneiderman had sued JP Morgan Chase for fraud stating that "Defendants committed multiple fraudulent and deceptive acts in promoting and selling its RMBS (Residential Mortgage-Backed Securities)."[24]

On October 11, 2013 JP Morgan announced that for the September quarter it had incurred a loss of $400 million compared with a profit of $5.7 billion for the same quarter in the previous year, as a result of the bank having to take a legal charge of $9.2 billion before tax.[25]

On October 23, 2013 US Federal authorities announced that they were prepared to take action in a criminal investigation of JP Morgan, suspecting that the bank turned a blind eye to its client Bernard L. Madoff's Ponzi scheme.[26] In common with many other central banks, the SARB maintains about two thirds of its foreign exchange in US dollars, the management of which is split between two New York banks. Currently just over half or R121 billion of South Africa's foreign exchange denominated in dollars is managed by JP Morgan Chase. This figure represents about 36% of total foreign reserves of R337 billion. On numerous occasions, including an e-mail sent on January 10, 2012 to Deputy Governor Daniel Mminele, which was not answered, I expressed my concerns about JP Morgan's custodianship in view of its appalling record of corporate governance. Such negligence by the SARB can only be described as reckless and irresponsible and requires urgent investigation by the Minister of Finance.

---

23 A. Damon and B. Gray JP Morgan scandal: The tip of the iceberg http://wsws.org/

24 www.businessinsider.com/ny-ag-sues-jp-morgan-for-fraud-over-mbs

25 *The Guardian*, October 12, 2013.

26 http://dealBook.nytimes.com/2013/10/23/madoff-action-seen-as-possible-for-jpmorgan/? R=0

Where Is All The Gold?

This refrain has been repeated for several years by concerned citizens of a number of countries, including Austria, Germany, the Netherlands[27] and Venezuela. The case of Germany, which has the world's second largest gold reserves of 3,395.5 tons, is of particular interest, as in terms of the *Geheimer Staatsvertrag* (Secret Treaty) of May 23, 1949 all German gold reserves would have to be lodged in the vaults of the US Federal Reserve Bank until 2099. Currently nearly half (1,536 tons) is believed to be still in New York, but they have never been audited and checked for either authenticity or weight, an omission which the *Bundesrechnungshof* (Federal Court of Auditors) has demanded that the Bundesbank (central bank) rectify. When a member of the Bundestag (lower house of parliament), Peter Gauweiler first tried to gain access to view the gold held in Frankfurt, he was refused entry on the grounds that there was a "lack of visiting rooms."[28] He eventually gained access in May 2012.

An attempt in May 2011 by a team of inspectors from the Bundesbank to inspect Germany's gold holdings in New York was thwarted in a similar fashion "in the interest of security and the control process"[29] and it was only permitted to view one of the nine chambers and a few bars. In early 2013 an agreement was reached between the Bundesbank and the US Federal Reserve Bank for the repatriation of 674 tons of gold over the period 2013 to 2020. The first annual consignment remitted consisted of only 37 tons instead of the contracted 84 tons. Of the 37 tons repatriated 32 tons came from the Banque de France and 5 tons from the US Federal Reserve Bank which was recast gold. This

---

27   M. Bouman, *Het Financiële Dagblad, Haal ons goud terug*, January 16, 2013.
28   http://www.zerohedge.com/news/2012-10-22/german-court-demands-bundesbank-audit-sovereign-gold-holdings
29   *Der Spiegel*, October 30, 2012.

Where Is All The Gold

Maverick Bavarian CSU politician Peter Gauweiler.

raises the strong suspicion that the original German gold has either been hypothecated or sold.[30] These events raise serious concerns as to the trustworthiness and probity of central banks, especially in view of the large number of gold plated tungsten bars in circulation.

South Africa is in a similar situation in that currently 90% of the country's gold reserves of 125 tons, which in total constitute about 12% of the overall reserves are kept at the Bank of England, apparently rent free. While there may have been a case for keeping gold reserves in a major financial centre when the gold exchange standard was in operation, since its dissolution on August 15, 1971 there exists no justifiable reason for persisting with what amounts to a violation of South Africa's sovereignty.

---

30   http://lionsdenmedia.hubpages.com/hub/Germany-Demands-Return-of-Gold-Held-by-US

Central banks usually "earmark" foreign gold holdings,[31] but the system is open to abuse. In August 2011 an audit of South Africa's gold holdings in London took place, but it is not clear whether an assurance of gold proof was obtained by the weighing of bars, examination of markings and the testing of bar cores. South Africa's gold holdings need to be returned to Pretoria *tout de suite*.

Can The Bank of England Be Trusted?

On May 7, 1999 Gordon Brown, Chancellor of the Exchequer, ordered the sale of 395 tons of gold, which represented over half of the United Kingdom's gold reserves of 690 tons. This was done at a time when the price of gold was starting to recover from previously depressed levels. The gold was sold from 1999 to 2002 and realised an average price of $275 per ounce, which is substantially below the current price of $1,400 per ounce and a peak of $1,895 reached in September 2011. These sales were apparently undertaken in order to diversify the United Kingdom's foreign exchange holdings into foreign currency deposits, and especially the euro. Inexplicably Brown announced this sale before it took place, which he said was part of his professed policy of "open government", but this announcement served only to reduce the price of gold. Furthermore the gold was sold at auction, instead of by private treaty, and resulted in even lower prices being achieved.

It has since been revealed that Brown was acting dishonestly. In 1999 Goldman Sachs and JP Morgan had shorted gold heavily to such an extent that if the gold price continued to rise, the former would have faced imminent bankruptcy. In order to prevent a banking crisis, the US Federal Reserve Bank and the

---

31   E.M. Josephson, *The "Federal" Reserve Conspiracy & Rockefellers*, Chedney Press, New York, 1968, 344.

Can The Bank of England Be Trusted

US Federal Reserve chairman Ben Bernanke and
British Prime Minister Gordon Brown.

Bank of England resolved to depress the price of gold. Brown was thus a patsy acting under orders given by the international bankers headed by the Rothschilds.[32] This was confirmed in a statement made by Eddie George, Governor of the Bank of England (1993-2003) in the presence of three witnesses when he spoke to Nicholas J. Morrell (CEO of Lonmin PLC) after the Washington Agreement on the gold price explosion in Sept/Oct 1999. Mr George said: "We looked into the abyss if the gold price rose further. A further rise would have taken down one or several trading houses, which might have taken down all the rest in their wake. Therefore at any price, at any cost, the central banks had to quell the price, manage it. It was very difficult to get the central banks to get the gold prices under control but we have now succeeded. The US Fed was very active in getting the gold price down so was the UK."[33]

---

32 T. Pascoe, Revealed: why Gordon Brown sold Britain's gold at a knock-down price, *The Daily Telegraph*, July 5, 2013. Blogs.telegraph.co.uk/finance/thomaspascoe/100018367/revealed-why-gordon-brown-sold-britains-gold-at-a-knock-down-price/#disqus_thread

33 T. Durden, March 24, 2010 www.zerohedge.com/article/did-gordon-brown-sell-uks-gold-keep-aig-rothschild-solvent-more-disclosures-how-ny-fed-

This unethical, if not criminal behaviour, was undertaken by the Bank of England in order to bail out insolvent, private banks at the expense of the public. It provides condemnatory proof as to why it is imprudent for South Africa, or for that matter any other country, to leave its gold[34] in the custody of the Bank of England.

Shareholder Dividends

Since 2009 the SARB has been making losses, but it continues, in contravention of Section 24(e) of the Act, to pay out annual dividends of R200,000 from reserves. The Act specifically states that a dividend at the rate of ten percent per annum on the paid-up share capital of the bank may only be paid "out of net profits." In support of this illegal payment, reliance was made on a foreign court decision, where a Spanish mining company was permitted to pay dividends out of its accumulated reserves.

In August 2003 when the shareholders approved a special resolution to pay an increased dividend out of the statutory reserves, it was pointed out that the Act would have to be amended to allow for the payment of dividends out of reserves. The author strongly opposed this illegal decision, which has resulted in the creation of an unhealthy precedent. Thus for dividends to be paid out of reserves, the Act has to be amended.

In May 2012 the Bank was obliged to deduct a 15% dividend tax from shareholders' dividends of 10 cents per share, notwithstanding the fact that (i) these dividends are fixed and in fact represent interest, (ii) the Bank has

---

manipulates-gold-prices

34 As at December 2012 the Bank of England held 5,790 tons of gold in custody, besides its own holdings of 310 tons.

not paid secondary company tax in the past and (iii) it is making losses. A request to the Commissioner of the South African Revenue Service for an exemption could easily have been made, as the annual loss to the fiscus is a trifling R30,000. However, the management of the SARB has little concern for the welfare of the Bank's shareholders, and this explains why so many of them are discontented and disillusioned.

Seigniorage

The SARB has incurred accumulated losses of over R7.2 billion since the 2010 financial year end, whereas during the governorship of Tito Mboweni (1999-2009), the Bank recorded profits of R10.7 billion. Furthermore as a result of Gill Marcus's incompetent handling of the Bank's affairs, the National Treasury has had to subsidise these escalating losses, with tax credits amounting to R2.42 billion for the 2010-2014 period.[35] Instead of contributing to the Fiscus the SARB has become in essence a ward of the state. The reasons provided by the Bank for these escalating losses are the negative differential between the rates of interest received on the Bank's foreign exchange holdings and the higher interest payable on rand deposits; the deemed necessity of having to purchase rands in the past in order to curb the appreciation of the external value of the rand; and the purchasing or "sterilising" of rands created as a result of overseas portfolio investments in order to reduce inflation. However, the underlying real reason why higher interest rates are required is that they are necessary in order to attract sufficient borrowers of government debt, which will help in bridging the budget deficit. Currently 37.2% of South Africa's government debt is held by foreigners. Since it stood at R294 billion in 1994, the national debt

---

35 The breakdown is as follows: 2009/10 R404 million, 2010/11 R451 million, 2011/12 R189 million, 2012/13 R581 million, 2013/14 R617 million.

has soared to current levels in excess of R1.4 trillion. If this trend continues with the likelihood that there will be no meaningful tapering in the foreseeable future of the US Federal Reserve Bank's quantitative easing programme, then the SARB faces *a fortiori* the prospect of bankruptcy by the end of the decade, as a result of its misguided policy of supporting the usurers at the expense of the taxpayers and the general public.

In February 2010 the author submitted a 72 page memorandum entitled *A Proposal to Secure the Permanent Funding of the South African Reserve Bank and the Provision of Low Interest Loans to Government, Municipalities and Parastatals* to Gill Marcus. She did not seem to grasp what it entailed and handed it to one of the Bank's economists. The memorandum, which included 11 appendices, provided an historical survey of central banking, including the foundation of the SARB, and examples of successful state banks both past and present. Proposed legislation, which would grant the SARB the exclusive right to create the nation's entire money supply at almost zero interest, would not only enable it to fund its operations permanently, but would provide an inestimable benefit to the people of South Africa in perpetuity. These benefits would include a liquidation of the national debt, much lower taxes, greatly enhanced prospects for economic growth and a concomitant large reduction in unemployment.

In a cursory reply of 2½ pages the Bank's economist condemned the concept of state banking, alleging that the proposals were "not viable" as "there are many examples of extremely unsuccessful state owned banks" (they were not cited) and "dangerous." He also claimed that the proposals by reversing "the elements in the Constitution[36] and in the South African Reserve Bank Act which provide for central

---

36 See Chapter VI, page 126 for an explanation as to why "the elements in the Constitution" which the SARB's economist relies on are hopelessly flawed.

Seigniorage

bank independence in the conduct of monetary policy, [would] undermine the central bank and destroy confidence in the South African monetary system." His final conclusion was that "unconventional, untried reforms that will lead to the collapse of the robust and respected financial system that South Africa has built up over generations, should not be contemplated (*sic passim*)."

The author subsequently spent three hours with the economist in an effort to find out why he had such a negative attitude. When the author reminded him of the highly successful examples of state banking in the past, he replied that that was all "history"[37] and told the author bluntly that he was "hostile" to the very idea of state banking. The author was thus unable to have the memorandum discussed at either a NEDCOM meeting or at a Board meeting and on the whim of an ill-informed economist the report was aborted. It is often claimed that the Reserve Bank is a "knowledge institution", but here is ample proof that it is suffused in nescience.

At the Board meeting held on 25 November 2010, the author informed the Board of a private Bill, which had been introduced in the House of Commons, England by Conservative member of parliament, Douglas Carswell. He had proposed 100 percent reserve requirements for all banks in the United Kingdom and the granting of powers to the Bank of England to extend credit. The author also drew attention to a recent speech[38] by the governor of the Bank of England, Sir Mervyn King, in which he contemplated a radical restructuring of the banking system. The author was immediately rebuked by Gill Marcus and accused of "hijacking the board". This abrasive and confrontational disposition is one of her more regrettable character traits.

---

37 For the past 25 years economics history has been seldom taught as a separate subject in universities and colleges, and if taught at all, usually forms part of a humanities curriculum.

38 *Banking: From Bagehot to Basel, and Back Again* The Second Bagehot lecture, Buttonwood gathering, New York City, October 25, 2010.

While chairman of ABSA Bank (2007-09) her continual sniping and aggressive and unpleasant behaviour towards Steve Booysen, group CEO of that bank, eventually resulted in his premature retirement in February 2009. Subsequent press reports confirmed that Steve Booysen had a "rocky relationship" with Gill Marcus and that "Marcus always wanted her way". It also transpired that she wanted to run the show and Booysen found that "extremely difficult".[39] Another example of her belligerent and arrogant manner occurred on May 27, 2010, when she was an invited guest speaker at the annual general meeting of the South African Institute of Chartered Accountants held at a hotel in Sandown, Johannesburg. In her opening remarks she insulted her hosts by saying, "I have a problem with this audience, you are all white and all male", disregarding the fact that the institute has been a non-racial organisation since its inception in 1894.

Academia

In the previous section attention was drawn to the ignorance of a senior economist at the SARB, who was unaware of how alternative banking systems function. For this blindness he cannot be blamed as he is a victim, as are almost all other economists throughout the world, of an educational system which permits only one form of finance to be taught, namely the orthodox model. Economics is akin to a religion where any deviation is deemed to be heretical and is swiftly punished by its high priests with excommunication.

This practice of brainwashing and indoctrination dates back to the early eighteenth century when the Bank of England was starting to spread its tentacles. A brother-

---

39 http://www.moneyweb.co.za/moneyweb-financial/absa-capital-ceo-out
    In the 2009 ABSA annual report Booysen's previous service was not acknowledged and appears to have been deliberately ignored. http://www.moneyweb.co.za/moneyweb-financial/no-thanks-for-steve-booysen-was-an-oversight

Ezra Pound (1885-1972) the celebrated American poet who played a leading role in exposing the financial crimes of the bankers in the twentieth century.

in-law of Sir Robert Walpole, Prime Minister of England (1721-42) was appointed to visit all colleges and universities to spread the gospel of fractional reserve banking based on a gold standard. In his preface to "A Fraudulent Standard", the renowned economist, Arthur Kitson, writes of a typical incident in the late nineteenth century as follows:

> "...I may mention that one of the unfortunate effects of that publication *A Scientific Solution of the Money Question* was to procure the dismissal of two well-known professors of Economics from their respective Colleges, at the instigation of their chief financial supporters, for having introduced and endorsed 'Kitson's heresies' – in their College lectures!" [40]

In a talk given on Radio Rome on March 15, 1942 the celebrated poet, Ezra Pound, who played a leading role in exposing the financial crimes of the bankers in the twentieth century, quoted from a text he had written in the spring of 1935, for a student quarterly of the University of Wisconsin as follows:

> "My generation was brought up ham ignorant of economics. History was taught with OMISSIONS of the most vital facts. Every page our generation read was overshadowed by usury. Not only was the press false, but every current idea had been warped by generations of antecedent perversion. The ACID TEST of public men today is plain and simple. MISTRUST any man, no matter how high in office who tries to get you AWAY from the questions. WHAT is money? Who makes it? How is it issued? Why can't the WHOLE people buy what the WHOLE people produces?" [41]

---

[40] A. Kitson, *A Fraudulent Standard*, Omni Publications, Hawthorne, California, 1972, (first published in 1917), vii.

[41] *"Ezra Pound Speaking" Radio Speeches of World War II*, Edited by L.W. Doob, Greenwood Press, Westport, Connecticut, 1978, 65.

Academia

On October 7-8, 2008 the author attended a course [42] at the Gordon Institute of Business Science in Johannesburg, which included as one of its topics a refresher course on Basel II,[43] ironically at the same time as the banking crisis was unfolding in New York. During the introductory lecture, a professor of 30 years' standing informed the assembled directors of a variety of South African banks, that banks make their profits from the difference in the lower interest rate that they pay depositors and the higher rate that they receive from borrowers. The author politely pointed out that the loans banks grant are created out of nothing by the simple method of leveraging up to 100% the value of their share capital and reserves. The astonishing reply he gave was: "Gosh, I had never thought of it that way." Afterwards Jurie Bester, former managing director of First National Bank came up to the author and said, "You have explained it exactly as it is."

At a seminar held at the SARB on July 1, 2011, Mr Jaime Caruana, general manager of the Bank for International Settlements (BIS), gave a lecture on "Central banking between past and future: Which way forward after the crisis?" the author asked him if the BIS had given any consideration to the state banking option, where by way of example, the Bank of North Dakota issued very low interest rate loans to farmers and for construction of public facilities, and as a result thereof there had been no financial crisis, a budget surplus, high economic growth and low unemployment. He replied that he had never heard of the Bank of North Dakota and that there must be "other reasons" for its prosperity.

---

42 Banking Board Leadership Programme: Risk Governance & Management Structures and Basel II Refresher & Operational Risk.

43 The Basel II Accord was adopted in June 2004 in an attempt to create for banks an international standard of adequate capital relative to credit, operational and market risks.

Inside the South African Reserve Bank

In June 2012 Professor David Miles, member of the Monetary Policy Committee, Bank of England made the following revealing statement, "The way monetary economics and banking is taught in many – maybe most – universities is very misleading."[44] This view was confirmed in a paper titled, *The Veil of Deception over Money: How Central Bankers and Textbooks Distort the Nature of Banking and Central Banking*, which was written by Norbert Häring, economics correspondent of the German business daily, *Handelsblatt*. He reveals how students (and the public) "are being intentionally and systematically misled about the nature of money and about the role of central bankers and by textbooks, like the ones of Krugman and Wells (2009) and Mankiw and Taylor (2011), that central banks have always been government institutions acting in the public interest. In reality, central banks' historical origin and role had more to do with the desire of private bankers to control and coordinate the process of private sector money creation. That most money is created in the private sector is something that central bankers like to gloss over and textbooks 'explain' in a distorted and unnecessarily convoluted way."[45]

In one of his concluding paragraphs, Häring highlighted the fact "that central bankers and prominent textbook authors share a desire to let us think that the creation of the vast majority of our means of payment by commercial banks for their own benefit is normal, harmless, without alternative and under the control of the central banks. Central bankers do so by avoiding any mention of private money creation or credit creation, and by pretending instead that central banks have a monopoly to create money. Textbook authors do so by distorting the process of money creation, using the rhetoric of the inappropriate loanable funds model. Their account of the role and legal status

---

44 See also J. Ryan-Collins, T. Greenham, R. Werner, A. Jackson, *Where Does Money Come From, A Guide to the UK Monetary and Banking System*, New Economics Foundation, London, 2012, 178 pp.

45 Real-World Economics Review, issue no. 63, April 2013, 1.

of central banks is highly selective and biased. Alternative monetary systems are hardly ever seriously discussed."[46]

Sovereign Wealth Fund

At the Board meeting held on November 30, 2011 the author introduced a memorandum for the establishment of a Sovereign Wealth Fund. Although South Africa's foreign exchange reserves of $50.3 billion[47] do not match up with those of some of the mostly resource-rich 48 nations which do have SWFs, there are long term benefits to be gained. These include higher returns on foreign exchange investments, stabilisation and reduction in volatility of government revenues, accumulation of savings for future generations and diversification from non-renewable commodity exports. The higher returns on invested assets would also reduce the SARB's losses.

Membership of barter organisations, such as the International Reciprocal Trade Association, would enable a portion of the foreign exchange reserves to be freed up for investment purposes. While barter does require a double coincidence of wants, it is a much cheaper form of trade, as there are no middlemen and financing costs involved. Although the memorandum was discussed, due to a lack of understanding, it was not pursued.

Monetary Policy Committee

The MPC meets about six times a year and on an *ad hoc* basis if circumstances require it to do so. Besides reviewing the state of the economy, its principal task is to adjust the level of interest rates through the so called repo or bank rate. Commentators and journalists frequently speculate as to

---

46 Ibid., 16.
47 As at April 30, 2013.

"What will the Governor do?", not realising that such powers to act are limited, as the forces influencing the economy are largely within the domain of the private bankers.

One of the major policies, which the MPC is responsible for implementing is inflation targeting, where attempts are made to restrict the rate of inflation[48] within a band, which has been determined by government. The band currently lies between 3% and 6% per annum. Australia was the first country to adopt inflation targeting in 1993 and currently 25 countries use this meaningless measurement. As will be explained shortly, inflation is simply a function of interest on money which has been created out of nothing, which interest is also created out of nothing and has not been backed by any productive labour. If South Africa had an honest money system, an inflation target of 0% would be eminently achievable. The MPC is nothing more than a publicity stunt, which serves to delude the public into believing that something is being done, when the reality is that the SARB is powerless to do anything effective over the long term.

Independence

One of the alleged pillars of central banking is its "independence". This "independence" is supposed to enable the central bankers of each nation to apply their minds in an objective manner when financial decisions have to be made, which ultimately will be for the benefit of the public. Furthermore it is alleged that this "independence" authorises central banks to pursue their principal purpose, which is to achieve stable growth and near full employment within a low inflation environment. On account of their fixation with price stability, these objectives are frequently

---

48 For political reasons inflation rates are continually distorted and understated. See www.shadowstats.com for proof that the real rates of inflation and unemployment in the United States are about three times higher than those reported by the US Bureau of Economic Analysis.

not achieved. As Professor Richard Werner of the University of Southampton has observed:

> "There are many other serious problems that central banks can create, such as recessions. In this case, inflation may be low, but the economy may suffer from large-scale unemployment induced purely by monetary policy. Central banks can also create deflation, which increases the real debt burden of borrowers, such as homeowners with mortgages. Again, by the measuring rod of low inflation, the central banks would have been doing a good job. But in reality they were not doing their job at all.[49]

> "The current power of central banks is difficult to reconcile with democracy. As long as central bankers continue to exert unchecked control over the quantity of credit and its allocation, they are the undisputed rulers of the economy. If they have such powers, they are likely to use them. This probably means the continuation of the boom-and-bust cycles engineered by central banks in pursuit of their goals. And these goals may be quite different from what we may naively assume. As long as there is no meaningful accountability, people's lives are but puppets in their credit game."[50]

Therefore the claim of "independence" must be deemed a travesty. At the conference of central bankers in Genoa in April/May 1922, Montagu Norman, governor of the Bank of England insisted that all central banks must be independent. But independent of whom, the State or the private banks? Clearly it is the former so that central banks will never have the ability to function as state banks creating the means of exchange free of debt and interest for the benefit of everyone.[51]

---

49 R.A. Werner, *Princes of the Yen*, M.E. Sharpe, New York, 2003, 237.
50 Ibid., 247.
51 For a lucid exposition of how to rectify the fraudulent money system, see 12 year

Instead of acting as the guardians of a nation's monetary system, the primary purpose of central banks is to protect[52] the monopoly which private banks have to create the money supply out of nothing.

One of the subsidiary purposes of a central bank's "independence" is to safeguard the private banks from the wrath of the public when the economy experiences its perennial problems of either unemployment, recession, inflation or deflation and to create the illusion of "power" in order to disguise where the real power lies, namely with the private banks. In this manner both the public and government are continually deceived as to the source of their torments and tribulations. The SARB has no contingency plans for a real crisis and when the next one occurs, as in 1929 and 1985, the usual chaos will prevail.

Inflation

Inflation[53] has been the scourge of mankind over the millennia, but its source and solution are very simple. As has already been expounded private banks are not intermediaries acting as a link between savers and borrowers, but creators of loans out of nothing matched with phony "deposits" for accounting purposes. What the private banks create is not

---

old Victoria Grant's speech on www.youtube.com/watch?v=sX7q9YF+Vc

52 S. Naidoo, Marcus gives big five banks a hand, *Mail & Guardian Business*, May 18, 2012, 1-2. This article describes why it is necessary to provide an emergency fund of R240 billion for the five commercial banks, which have a potential mismatch between short term funding and long term lending in terms of the Basel III Accord, which comes into force in 2019. This fund may be inadequate, as the Banking Association of South Africa has warned that the liquidity gap could be as high as R900 billion. The banks are required to pay an upfront commission or fee of R700 million as well as interest paid on any amounts drawn down in the future, all of which will be ultimately borne by the consumer.

53 J.J. Rossouw, *Inflation in South Africa 1921 to 2006 History Measurement and Credibility*, unpublished doctoral thesis, School of Development Studies, University of KwaZulu-Natal, August 1, 2007. For a history of inflation, see Chapter 2 Literature Review.

Inflation

money, but debt, which does not have a legal tender status and is immediately destroyed when the debt is repaid.

When a commercial bank creates a loan, it does not create the interest to be paid on it. Additional loans have to be created to pay the interest, which is for a non-productive purpose and is not backed by labour. This interest contributes to a rising money supply and a continuing cycle of re-borrowing until the interest can no longer be paid, the debt is reneged and the economy slides into recession/depression. Such a systematically expanding debt is called a geometric progression, which taken to the limit will become infinite. The summation of all infinite series or progressions can be expressed by an equation. Thus in this particular progression of debt arising from the application of compound interest, the equation is exponential and eventually will become unsustainable.

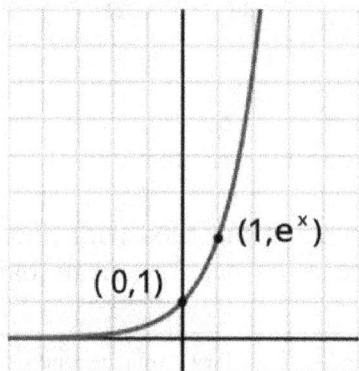

The natural exponential function

The above graph explains what an exponential equation looks like, where "e" is the base of the natural logarithmic system and has a numerical value of 2.718... The bottom axis is the time over which the debt matures. The vertical axis represents the accumulation of debt. In the usury system growth of debt + interest accelerates with time and there is a shorter and shorter period in which to alleviate the problem.

Inside the South African Reserve Bank

Winston Churchill and Jewish financier Bernard Baruch adviser and confidant to six US presidents.

As at June 2014 global debt exceeded $223 trillion[54], while government debt stood at $100 trillion, a 42.6% increase from $70 trillion in mid-2007, and has now grown to the point where it has surpassed the knee of the exponential curve at (1,e) and is shooting up asymptotically to the vertical. This parabolic curve of debt + interest proves that a financial system based on debt and usury will eventually implode.

According to Dr Albert A. Bartlett, Professor of Physics at the University of Colorado (Boulder) this mathematical certainty has been largely ignored because "The greatest shortcoming of the human race is our inability to understand the exponential function."

---

54 http://theeconomiccollapseblog.com/archives/12-numbers-about-the-global-financial-ponzi-scheme-that-should-be-burned-into-your-brain

UBUNTU Party[55]

In March 2014 the author teamed up with the UBUNTU Party which was standing in the 2014 South African general election. Ubuntu is an ancient African word which means human kindness or humanity to others. I was nominated as the second candidate on the parliamentary list and assisted the party in drafting its economic and financial policies. For the first time in its history the UBUNTU Party offered the electorate of South Africa, a proposal to set up a People's Bank on state banking lines. This bank would create the nation's money supply free of debt and interest. The benefits flowing from a People's Bank would enable all government infrastructure to be financed free of interest, agricultural loans at 0% plus a small handling fee, as practised in North Dakota, home loans at 0% plus a small handling fee, free electricity for domestic consumers as a result of the electricity utility, Eskom, no longer having to pay interest on its loans, lower taxes, zero inflation and near full employment.

---

55   http://www.ubuntuparty.org.za/

The UBUNTU Party launched a sophisticated publicity campaign using leaflets, posters, radio advertising in several indigenous languages, radio interviews, a mobi-fun cell phone campaign, e-mails, t-shirts, YouTube clips and a trailer which was parked in several parts of Johannesburg. In addition to its existing membership of 20,000, the party received thousands of offers of support and help, and built up a supporters' base of almost one million. Included in this figure were the 160,000 supporters of the New Economics Rights Alliance, many of whose members are victims of banking malpractices such as home and furniture repossessions, extortionate interest rates, forged court orders and stolen title deeds. The party was thus assured of at least 100,000 votes or two seats in parliament. In the event the party only received 8,234 votes.

It became apparent that something was seriously wrong when one of the party agents, who observed the counting of the international votes – the UBUNTU Party has a strong following overseas – reported that the party had received a quarter of the 18,132 votes cast (i.e. 4,500), but only 16 votes were recorded on the scanned receipt.

Since "democratic" elections were first introduced in 1994, the Independent Election Commission has been rigging results on a regular basis in favour of the ANC. This was confirmed in an article at that time in the Dutch newspaper, *Nederlands Dagblad* 'Verkiezingen Zuid-Afrika oneerlijk' (Elections – South Africa dishonest) by former president F.W. de Klerk, who said that over one million ballot papers in favour of the ANC had been stuffed in piles into ballot boxes. 20 years later it is apparent that not much has changed, when the head of the Independent Electoral Commission, whose ironic slogan is "ensuring free and fair elections", Mrs Pansy Tlakula, was accused by National Treasury of having been involved in corruption and fraud regarding the lease of the IEC's new building.[56]

---

56   http://udm.org.za/iec-lease-agreement-scandal-iec-paying-for-commission-chairpersons-legal-costs/

UBUNTU Party

According to an article in the *Mail & Guardian*[57] vote rigging in the 2014 election was rampant, particularly in the province of Gauteng. When it became clear that the ANC was slipping below the 50% barrier, counting was delayed for over 24 hours in order to manipulate the results in its favour. Independent observers have revealed that many counting slips were not signed off by the counting officer, or where they had been, they were not signed by a party agent. There were results which had been signed off by auditors, but differed enormously from the scanned slips. There were also huge differences in the votes cast by the opposition parties on the national and provincial lists, which is a clear indication that there had been tampering with the ballot papers. The author has little doubt who was ultimately responsible for this outrage perpetrated against the UBUNTU Party, and the circumstantial evidence together with its track record of criminal intent and behaviour in the past points only in one direction, viz. the South African Reserve Bank.

---

57   http://mg-co-za/article/2014-05-10-gauteng-discrepancies-on-audited-results-anger-parties?htm

Chapter VI

From the time I took office as Chancellor of the Exchequer (1852) I began to learn that the State held, in face of the Bank [of England] and the City, an essentially false position as to finance...The hinge of the whole situation was this: the Government itself was not to be a substantive power in matters of finance, but was to leave the Money Power supreme and unquestioned.

– William Ewart Gladstone,
Prime Minister of England.

The Solution: The State Bank of the Republic of South Africa

The empirical evidence exhibited in the histories of the highly successful state banks of Australia, France, Germany, Italy, Japan and Russia[1], as well as the recent confirmation of the viability of full reserve banking and the tremendous advantages to be derived there from, provided by the IMF researchers, Jaromir Benes and Michael Kumhoff, who reappraised Professor Irving Fisher's *Chicago Plan*[2], proves beyond all doubt that central banks need to be reformed and converted into government owned and controlled monopolies, if the impending economic and demographic collapse is to be averted. There have been frequent calls, particularly by trade unions, that the SARB should be nationalised. However, nationalisation will not make the slightest difference, unless the system is changed and the reconstituted bank falls under the direct control of the Treasury.

---

1 S. M. Goodson, *A History of Central Banking and the Enslavement of Mankind*, Black House Publishing, London, 2014, 214 pp.

2 *The Chicago Plan*, issued on March 16, 1933 advocated that the state should create the nation's money supply and that private banks should operate as full reserve banks. Using mathematical principles, Fisher was able to prove that full employment would be the result, business cycles would be abolished and inflation would be reduced and remain at zero.

The State Bank of the Republic of South Africa

There is a popular misconception that South Africa has one of the best and most comprehensive constitutions in the world, which safeguards the rights of individuals and enables each person to realise his/her aspirations in a society unfettered by any form of prejudice or discrimination. This is the theory, but the reality is unfortunately the opposite.

In 2012 the author discussed the section of the Constitution which deals with the SARB (Sections 223-225) with the constitutional lawyer, Dr Mario Oriani-Ambrosini [3], who composed it. He said that at that time he had concerns when drafting it and in retrospect has agreed that he made an error of judgement and that as a result thereof the Constitution is a fatally flawed document.

It states in its preamble that one of the purposes of the Constitution is to enable South Africa "to take its rightful place as a sovereign state in the family of nations".[4] For any nation to make the claim that it possesses absolute sovereignty, as established at the Treaty of Westphalia in 1648, four additional and critical factors need to be present.

(i) Monetary independence
(ii) Food independence [5]
(iii) Energy independence
(iv) Military independence [6]

---

3   Dr M. G. R. Oriani-Ambrosini was largely responsible for the drafting of the South African Constitution. He served as legal adviser to Prince Mangosuthu Buthelezi, who has written the Foreward to the companion volume, *A History of Central Banking and the Enslavement of Mankind*, during South Africa's constitutional negotiations in the early 1990s and as sole Cabinet Adviser to Prince Buthelezi when the latter was Minister of Home Affairs (1994-2004). Oriani-Ambrosini was an Inkatha Freedom Party member of parliament (2009-2014) and during his membership served on seven parliamentary committees.

4   Act 108 of 1996.

5   Since 2009 South Africa has been a net importer of food. According to the Global Food Security Index of the *Economist Intelligence Unit* of July 2012, South Africa had dropped to a lowly rated figure of 40.

6   Since abandoning its nuclear weapons programme in 1989, South Africa has

Inside the South African Reserve Bank

Up to 1994 the last three categories of independence were existent, but since the first European settlement commenced 362 years ago in 1652, South Africa has never been sovereign in its financial affairs. It remains a vassal state right up to the present day, and as with almost all other countries of the world, is little more than an administrative convenience of the international bankers. By allowing, through the SARB, private bankers the right to create the nation's money supply as an interest-bearing debt, the supreme sovereignty of the state has been sacrificed and permanently undermined. As has already been mentioned in Chapter I the granting by legislation in 1920 of the right to create the people's means of exchange to commercial banks was **an act of treason.**

The solution to this problem is simple and straightforward. It requires the repeal of Sections 223-225 of the Constitution and the South African Reserve Bank Act, Act 90 of 1989 as amended and the implementation of The Monetary Reform Act. Sections 223-225 of Chapter 13: Finance read as follows:

Central Bank Establishment

223. The South African Reserve Bank is the central bank of the Republic of South Africa and is regulated in terms of an Act of Parliament.

---

acquired some advanced weaponry at a cost of in excess of R60 billion. (The original government estimate was R29.9 billion, but it may have cost as much as R100 billion. This upper range may be found in A. Feinstein, *After the Party*, Jonathan Ball Publishers, Jeppestown, Johannesburg, 2007, 273.) A fair portion of this inflated cost was required to cover the substantial bribes and commissions paid to government ministers and their agents. Most of this equipment has not been deployed because of a lack of skilled personnel. For example for 26 Gripen aircraft, of which four are still in their original packing at the Saab factory in Linkoping, Sweden, there are believed to be only 6 trained pilots, none of whom has fighter pilot status. Lack of aviation fuel is another constraint. For a brief summary of the debacle, which has taken place in the navy, see S. Goodson, The Sinking of the South African Navy, *Impact,* Aug./Sept. 2010.

The State Bank of the Republic of South Africa

224. (1) The primary object of the South African Reserve Bank is to protect the value of the currency in the interest of balanced and sustainable economic growth in the Republic.

(2) The South African Reserve Bank in pursuit of its primary object, must perform its functions independently and without fear, favour or prejudice, but there must be regular consultation between the bank and the Cabinet member responsible for national financial matters.

Powers and Functions

225 The powers and functions of the South African Reserve Bank are those customarily exercised and performed by central banks, which powers and functions must be exercised or performed subject to the Conditions prescribed in terms of that Act.

As has already been explained in the previous chapter the SARB has failed to achieve any of these objectives throughout the 93 years of its existence, and has been directly responsible for the currency, the rand, having lost over 99.5% of its purchasing power, countless booms and busts and the enslavement of the people by not providing the nation's money supply on a debt free and interest free basis. Moreover, it can be confidently stated that under the current monetary regime these objectives will never be realised.

Sections 223-225 will thus need to be replaced by the following clauses.[7]

(i)   Parliament will have the sole and exclusive power to create any form of money – physical or electronic – free of debt and interest.

(ii) The power to create the nation's money supply will

---

7   See Appendix II for full text.

vest in a Monetary Trusteeship, consisting of seven to eleven independent persons, who are appointed by and responsible solely to Parliament.

(iii) The Monetary trusteeship will meet at least once a month and will have at its disposal the full co-operation of the Minister of Finance, the Treasury and the State Bank of the Republic of South Africa.

(iv) The Minister of Finance together with other related agencies will be responsible for executing the directives of The Monetary Trusteeship.

(v) The volume of emission will be determined by a price index as computed by Statistics South Africa, which will include changes in production, costs and demographic factors.

(vi) New money will be paid into the economy by the Treasury and withdrawn, when necessary, in order to maintain a stable price level by means of temporary taxation.

The Monetary Reform Act[8] will provide for the nationalisation of money, but not the banking system. It will include *inter alia* the following provisions.

(i) The statutory requirement that all commercial banks and other lending institutions hold at all times 100% reserves.

(ii) The retirement of the National Debt.[9]

(iii) Permanent stabilisation of the money supply.

(iv) The establishment of a Monetary Trusteeship, which is responsible for the future growth of a permanent and stable money supply.

(v) Withdrawal from all international banks and their related agencies.

---

8   See Appendix II for full text.
9   In the 2013/14 national budget of R1.1492 trillion an amount of R1.768 billion or 15.3% was allocated to interest on government loans. In the national accounts it is furtively described as "Other".

The State Bank of the Republic of South Africa

(vi) Establishment of a Foreign Exchange Stabilisation Fund.

In terms of this legislation there will be far greater transparency. Meetings of the Monetary Trusteeship will be broadcast live and posted on its website, while meetings of the State Bank will be recorded and corrected minutes posted on the bank's website.[10] Three members of civil society such as representatives of agricultural unions, business chambers, trade unions etc. will be allowed to attend meetings of the bank on a rotational basis. As the bank will now be creating the people's money they will be entitled to know how it is being managed. Once this legislation has been adopted and implemented, it will be possible to achieve the following objectives in perpetuity.

(i) Abolition of income tax and reduction in VAT. (Government, provinces, municipalities and parastatals will no longer have to pay interest on their bonds)

(ii) Zero inflation. (It will no longer be necessary to expand the money supply for payment of interest which is inflationary).

(iii) Termination of business cycles.

(iv) Full employment (Those unemployed will be granted a living wage).

(v) Government's budgetary needs financed free of debt and interest.

(vi) Agricultural loans at zero interest + a small handling charge.

(vii) Housing loans at zero interest + a small handling charge.

(viii) Housing of the entire population within a five year period.[11]

---

10 The *Sveriges Riksbank* (Swedish Central Bank) releases the minutes of its Monetary Policy meetings to the public.

11 According to the 2011 census 1.2 million households are recorded as "informal" dwellings and there are 712,956 backyard shacks. These

(ix) A once-off one third reduction in the prices of goods and services, which includes electricity,[12] once all interest payments via the distribution channel have been phased out.

(x) Permanent prosperity.

Objective no. (vii) will have the greatest immediate impact. Currently home owners with bonds expend about 46.5% of their after tax income on servicing and repaying their home loans.[13] Mortgages constitute approximately 50% of all loans issued by private banks. The introduction of zero interest housing loans plus a small handling charge will obviously have a negative effect on the profitability of commercial banks, but it needs to be borne in mind that over half of their profits are derived from non-lending activities. Furthermore the heightened level of economic activity will assist in compensating for this loss of income, notwithstanding the fact that all monies lent in future will consist of existing money, issued by the state free of debt and interest. Competition between commercial banks and the efficient allocation of capital will remain intact.

In an article in the *SA Real Estate Investor* of May 2011, 'Introducing the Sovereign Man Breaking free from financial checkmate', Robert Vivian, Professor of Finance and Insurance at the School of Economic and Business Sciences at the University of the Witwatersrand endorses this important aspect of monetary reform.

The fourth last paragraph reads as follows:

---

structures house over 6,000,000 persons of whom 1,000,000 are whites.
12   A German study in 2009 revealed that 30% to 50% of everything purchased consists of interest. *The Free Press*, November 13, 2009, 4.
13   http://www.mg.co.za/article/2011-01-13-joburg-pe-most-affordable-for-home-buyers

Nevertheless, the operation of the global banking system raises a number of fundamental issues. As just one example, the interest charged by banks must be called into question.

"Money" loaned is "created" out of nothing, and the bank does not loan its own money to the borrower, why is interest charged by the bank? "A management fee payable to the bank managing the system seems more appropriate," comments Professor Vivian.

The proposed banking amendments will benefit not only homeowners, but all classes of borrowers whether they are government, entrepreneurs, farmers, or workers. The abandonment of debt slavery will enable not only the great wealth of this nation to be spread more evenly, it will also ensure the permanent eradication of poverty.

However, the path to economic revival, social upliftment and enduring prosperity can only be achieved if there is a complete overhaul of the financial system – there is no other methodology! This alternative monetary system has been precisely delineated and empirically proven to be highly successful in the past. It is incumbent on each one of us to apprise ourselves of this system's contents and the many benefits which it contains; and furthermore, spread far and wide its message of hope and salvation which can regenerate society for the benefit of all its citizens.

Appendix I

How Money is Created

Money consists of three types, which are used as mediums for the exchange of goods and services. They are coins, banknotes and credit. All three constitute what is known as the money supply.

1) Coins and Bank Notes.
Bank notes have been produced and issued since 1922 by the South African Reserve Bank (SARB). Before 1922 commercial banks issued bank notes for domestic use. The cost of printing a bank note varies between 55 cents and 70 cents depending on the denomination. It is more expensive to print higher denomination notes because of the extra paper, ink and security features.

The SARB assumed responsibility for the minting of coins in 1988. Previously the mint was owned by government. The cost of minting coins varies according to their metallic content and size. Commercial banks pay for these bank notes and coins and their accounts are credited when they return worn/damaged bank notes and coins.

The SARB invests the money it receives from commercial banks and the interest received on such investment is called seigniorage. It is used to fund the operations of the central bank. 10% of profits after taxation are retained and a fixed dividend of R200,000 per annum is paid to the SARB's shareholders less a 15% dividend tax. The balance of profits is paid over to the state. Bank notes provide 5-6% of the money supply. 60 years ago this figure was as high as 25%. This reduction in its relative proportion may be ascribed to advances in technology.

How Money is Created

2) Credit.

The commercial banks create the remaining 94-95% of the money supply by allowing borrowers, who have provided the requisite security or collateral in the case of secured loans, to withdraw an agreed amount relative to the amount of share capital and reserves, which commercial banks have invested in property, short term assets, such as cash and 90 day treasury bills and long term assets, principally government bonds.

Formerly, the SARB would issue directives as to the amount of reserves required relative to the duration of the loan, the volume of credit advanced and the maximum growth rate at which credit extension could increase. This system was abolished in September 1980. Currently the SARB prescribes only the level of reserves (reserve requirements) that commercial banks must hold on deposit at the central bank.

The percentage of share capital and overall reserves, which commercial banks must maintain, is governed by regulations prescribed by the Bank for International Settlements in Basel, Switzerland and the Registrar of Banks. At present it is 10% and will be raised in terms of the Basel III agreement to 14% by 2019. However, South African commercial banks already exceed this recommended level and their share capital and reserves or capital adequacy ratio stand at 15.6%[1] of all outstanding loans. It should be noted that the 14% mark is an overall percentage and that for property loans, for example, only 7% of loans provided need to be covered by reserves.

From the aforesaid it will be perceived that commercial banks are not quasi borrowers and lenders of money, but creators of money out of nothing, their capacity to do

---

1   As at December 2013, *Financial Stability Review*, SARB, March 2014, 15.

so being limited only to their holdings of share capital and reserves, and deposits, which they have the ability to leverage up. Thus when a loan is granted there is an increase in the money supply. On the other hand when a loan is repaid, money is destroyed and there is a decrease in the supply. This is known as the fractional reserve banking system. It may be contrasted with the full reserve banking system, where banks are only able to lend out money which they have received as deposits. Under this system the responsibility for creating the money supply (out of nothing) at nominal or zero interest rates resides exclusively with a state bank as was the case with the German Reichsbank (1933-1945), the Banca d'Italia (1936-1943) and the Bank of Japan (1931-1945).

On these loans, which represent money created with the backing of share capital, reserves and deposits, banks charge interest. This interest is used to pay interest on deposits and to cover operational expenses. A large portion of this interest received on money which the banks have created out of nothing may be construed as being a form of seigniorage. The banks other important source of income is the fees charged on various transactions. The interest rate charged is influenced by the repo rate (formerly known as the bank rate), currently standing at 5.75% per annum, which is set by the SARB and altered from time to time, as dictated by circumstances, at Monetary Policy Committee meetings. The maximum rate of interest, which may be levied by commercial banks on loans, is determined by the Usury Act, Act No. 73 of 1968. In terms of the National Credit Act, Act No.34 of 2005 the *in duplum* rule is applicable, viz. that the total interest levied may not exceed the amount loaned.

Appendix II

Proposed Legislation Amendment To The Constitution of the Republic of South Africa

CHAPTER 13
FINANCE

Sections 223-225 to be replaced by the following heading and clauses:

MONETARY TRUSTEESHIP AND STATE CENTRAL BANK

(i) Parliament shall have the sole power to issue (i.e. create) money in any form, which money will be issued debt-free and interest-free.

(ii) The power to create money shall ultimately vest in a Monetary Trusteeship (a body similar to the Constitutional Court), which body shall comprise of no fewer than seven (7) and no more than eleven (11) competent and trustworthy individuals, independent of all private interests, and appointed by the National Assembly to be answerable to it on a regular basis or as financial and/or national circumstances may demand.

(iii) The Monetary Trusteeship shall meet once a month, as well as at other times as and when circumstances may require it to do so, in order to exercise its duties of oversight over the monetary soundness of the State and execution of (ii) *supra*, for which purpose the full co-operation by the Minister of Finance and the various agencies and resources under his control shall be made available to this body.

Proposed Legislation

(iv) The executive functions for purposes of (i) *supra*, shall resort under the Minister of Finance working through the agencies of the Department of Finance, the Treasury; and the reconstituted South African Reserve Bank.

(v) The volume of emission, (or the amount to be withdrawn, as the case may be), as also the total amount of money in circulation, shall be determined by a price index, and the value thereof shall, as far as is practicable, be kept at a stable level so as to avoid prolonged periods of either excessive abundance or shortage.

(vi) New additional money put into circulation, together with such money withdrawn from circulation, as the case may be, by way of taxes, levies, licences, etc., shall pay for expenses of the State and thereby, in the first place abolish the need to levy income and/or expenditure taxes on individuals, small and medium sized businesses, or any other class of person or activity as may be decided upon at the discretion of the Minister of Finance and the Monetary Trusteeship, and in the second place, abolish, as and when deemed practicable, any other forms of taxation levied on the citizens of the Republic of South Africa.

(vii) No debt, public or private, shall be enforceable at law, unless there is adequate provision for amortisation within the time during which the real value created by the loan will have been amortised and all such loans shall stipulate a maximum period of repayment.

Statutes of the Republic of South Africa - Finance

Monetary Reform Act

[Date of Assent to be proclaimed]
[Date of Commencement to be proclaimed]
(English text to be signed by the President)

ACT

To restore confidence in and governmental control over money and credit, to stabilise the money supply and price level, to establish full-reserve banking, to retire the national debt, to repeal conflicting Acts, to withdraw from international banks, to restore political accountability for monetary policy, and to remove the causes of economic recessions and depressions.

BE IT ENACTED by the Parliament of the Republic of South Africa as follows:-

Section 1. Short Title.

This Act may be cited as the Monetary Reform Act.

Section 2. Implementation.

This Act shall be implemented over a transition period of one year and eight months, commencing thirty days after the date of the enactment of this Act.

Section 3. One Hundred Percent (100%) Reserve Requirement.

The Reserve Requirement ratio for financial institutions is hereby raised in equal monthly increments of five percent (5%) to one hundred percent (100%) during the said transition period. No existing reserve requirements shall be reduced, but shall be increased as the overall Reserve Requirement ratio incremental increase surpasses them. No waivers or exceptions shall be granted.

Monetary Reform Act

Section 4. Retiring The National Debt.

The Minister of Finance is hereby authorised and directed to purchase, in open market operations or otherwise as the case may be, all outstanding Republic of South Africa Loan Stock held by the public with South African Notes. Thereby the net National Debt is to be completely retired and replaced with South African Notes.

Section 5. Stable Money Supply.

The Minister of Finance is hereby authorised and directed to time and apportion the purchase of Republic of South Africa Loan Stock and other government debt securities held by the public, and the issuance of South African Notes and the creation of Treasury Deposits to the rate of the Reserve Requirement ratio increases made pursuant to this Act, in order to keep the money supply (calculated to include the monetary substitutions ~ provided for herein) stable, except as is provided in section 6, *infra*.

Section 6. Future Monetary Growth.

Beginning with the transition year period, and thereafter on an annual basis, the total rand amount of South African Notes (as defined *supra* - i.e. the sum of outstanding currency plus Treasury Deposits) outstanding shall be increased by the Treasury according to the increase in the price index as determined by Statistics South Africa. The computation of the price index shall include, but shall not be limited to, the following factors: (a) basic raw material prices; (b) finished goods produced; (c) population size, growth and distribution; (d) the form and extent of economic, demographic and societal distortions; and (e) any other factors which may from time to time become evident.

The amount of new money thus created shall be paid into the economy by the Treasury, first to retire (or purchase) any remaining non-marketable government debt and thereafter, pursuant to appropriation by Parliament, to pay for goods, services, grants or interest as required by the State. Any such new money not appropriated (i.e. allocated for expenditure) by Parliament during any particular financial year, shall be held over to be utilised in a subsequent year, or years as the case may be, thereby reducing the need for additional money in such subsequent year or years.

Section 7. Full-Reserve Banks.

After the transition period, institutions using the word bank in their name or title, may not engage in lending, except that their depositors' capital may be invested or loaned on the open market, but may charge fees and commissions for their services and may invest in Treasury Deposit accounts. These full-reserve; one hundred percent (100%) reserve, deposit, or cheque, banks as they, exclusively, may also be called, shall treat deposits received as trust funds held on behalf of depositors. After the end of the transition period, for every rand deposited, banks must have a rand of South African Notes on hand, or invested in a Treasury Deposit account, or invested with clients of such banks. Banks may be clients of other banks. All bank deposits shall be in demand accounts and/or accounted for in the books of the bank in a satisfactory manner and with due diligence, with oversight by relevant branches of the State permitted at any and all times. Banks shall be free to pay any rate of interest on accounts. Only bank deposits may be transferable by cheque, credit card, electronic transfer, or any substitute thereof. Other than oversight in the interests of the public at large, Government shall have nothing to do with the retail merchandising of money and this shall remain the domain of banks with full (100%) reserves, which banks may be privately owned and controlled.

Section 8. Treasury Deposits.

Funds placed in Treasury Deposits shall be utilised by the Minister of Finance pursuant to appropriation by

Monetary Reform Act

Parliament, i.e. to pay for goods, services, grants or interest as required by the State from time to time. Any such funds received by the State in excess of expenditure not funded by tax revenues during any particular financial year, shall be held over to be utilised in a subsequent year, or years as the case may be, thereby reducing the need for additional finance in such subsequent year or years.

Withdrawals of Treasury Deposits in excess of receipts in any particular financial year shall be funded by monetary growth as provided in section 6 *supra*.

Section 9. Interest.

The initial rate of interest payable on Treasury Deposits shall be equal to the average yield on three-month Treasury bills during the preceding quarter. Thereafter it shall be adjusted quarterly in accordance with changes in the average yield of ninety (90) day commercial paper over the preceding quarter.

Section 10. Repeal Of Conflicting Act.

The South African Reserve Bank Act, Act No. 90 of 1989 as amended, is hereby repealed, effective at the end of the transition period. All South African Reserve Bank Deposits shall be transferred to the Treasury at the end of the transition period.

From the effective date of this Act, and during the transition period, the South African Reserve Bank shall not engage in open market transactions, nor change the Repo rate, nor alter any reserve requirements, nor otherwise alter any money aggregate, nor transfer, dispose of, nor move any gold in either their physical or legal possession, except as provided for in this Act, contrary provision of the South African Reserve Bank Act or other statutes notwithstanding.

Section 11. Reconstituted South African Reserve Bank.

The department of the Treasury dealing with the requirements of this Act shall be known as the State Bank of the Republic of South Africa.

Section 12. Penalties.

After the transition period, no person may loan, create credit or liabilities on demand or transferable by cheque, credit card or electronic transfer without one hundred percent (100%) reserves of South African Notes, rand for rand, and as provided for in this Act, for any such amounts. Violation of this provision will subject the violator to criminal penalties or to civil penalties for fraud, or both. Fines shall not exceed three times the rand amount of the violation, or imprisonment up to twenty five (25) years, or both.

Section 13. Withdrawal From International Banks.

It is hereby declared as a matter of statutory law that membership and/or participation of the Republic of South Africa or its agencies, or of the South African Reserve Bank, or any officer or employee thereof, with the Bank for International Settlements, the International Monetary Fund, the World Bank, and all other international banks, is inconsistent with and in direct conflict with the purposes of this Act. This provision shall apply to equal extent in respect of the reconstituted South African Reserve Bank.

The Minister of Finance is hereby authorised and directed to take such steps as may be necessary to withdraw the Republic of South Africa from all participation and membership in the Bank for International Settlements, the International Monetary Fund, the World Bank and all other international banks in an orderly manner, and, if practicable, in a period not to exceed one year from the effective date of this Act, and to recover the original and any subsequent South African subscriptions, contributions and quotas to such organisations not already fully and lawfully expended, whether in the form of gold, deposits, currency or otherwise.

Monetary Reform Act

Section 14. Foreign Exchange.

The Minister of Finance is hereby authorised and directed to enact regulations allowing the external rate of exchange of the rand to fluctuate in sympathy with foreign price fluctuations (i.e. in accordance with their respective purchasing powers), for which purpose a Foreign Exchange Stabilisation Fund shall be maintained to counterbalance such fluctuations. The Foreign Exchange Stabilisation Fund book shall record, account for, and house, as far as is practicable, all foreign reserves.

Banks, foreign currency exchange entities, and the public at large shall be under obligation to deposit any and all foreign capital holdings over one hundred thousand rand (R100,000) in the case of banks and foreign currency exchanges, and five thousand rand (R5,000) in the case of private individuals, (or such amounts as may from time to time be advised by the Minister of Finance by way of a notification in the Government Gazette), with the Foreign Exchange Stabilisation Fund. Banks and foreign currency exchange entities shall report their holdings of foreign currency on a weekly basis to the reconstituted South African Reserve Bank.

Foreign currency exchange entities shall include, but shall not be limited to, businesses established to act as currency exchangers (e.g. Bureaux de Change) and businesses established to act as travel agents. Failure to report accurately, fully and within the stipulated time, on foreign currency holdings shall be a criminal offence subject to a fine not exceeding ten million rands (R10,000,000) in the case of businesses, one hundred thousand rands (R100,000) in the case of individuals, or imprisonment up to ten (10) years, or both, as the case may be.

The Minister of Finance shall enact such regulations in order (1) to keep the stable internal domestic price level established by this Act unaffected by foreign exchange rate fluctuations, and (2) to maintain the importation and exportation of capital in equilibrium. In no instance shall foreign exchange rates be allowed to alter the rate of monetary growth set forth in section 6, *supra*.

In any period, in which the to be established Exchange Stabilisation Fund and foreign currency reserves are inadequate to maintain equilibrium in capital flow, the Minister of Finance is hereby authorised and directed to restrict any imbalanced inflow of rands to an amount equal to the monetary growth for such period (as set forth in Section 6, *supra*), which monetary growth shall be thus funded; and to prohibit any imbalanced outflow of rands. Imbalances in excess of such amounts must first be chronologically booked for subsequent exchange as soon as free markets restore the equilibrium necessary for the exchanges to occur.

The Minister of Finance shall issue regulations to establish a Forward Foreign Exchange Book, open to public inspection by interested and affected parties, of all contracted future foreign exchange transactions and obligations, in order to facilitate such exchanges. Such exchanges must be assigned by the Minister of Finance on a "first come, first served" basis in order to guarantee foreign exchange availability.

Section 15. Appropriations.

The Minister of Finance is hereby authorised and directed to establish Treasury Deposits convertible to South African Notes on demand, sufficient to accomplish the provisions of this Act.

Section 16. Severability.

If any provision of this Act, amendments made by this Act, or the application of such provisions or amendments to any person or circumstance, shall be held to be unconstitutional, the remainder of this Act, the amendments made by this Act, and the application of the provisions of such to any person or circumstance, shall not be affected thereby.

Appendix III

Frequently Asked Questions

1) *Who will own the State Bank?* The people and the State.

2) *Who will have overall responsibility for the running of the State Bank?* The Monetary Trusteeship, an organ of Parliament.

3) *Who will manage the State Bank on a day to day basis?* The Treasury.

4) *How will the State Bank fund current government expenditure?* By paying newly created money into the economy on a planned budget.

5) *How will the State Bank fund government capital expenditure?* By issuing zero interest bonds to organisations such as the Public Works Department, Eskom and Spoornet.

6) *At what rate will the money supply expand?* The rate of increase will be reviewed monthly and will be subject to changes in the various price indices, demographic changes and increases/decreases in productivity.

7) *Will the private banks be nationalised?* No, only the money supply will be nationalised. Full reserve banks will continue to compete with each other and efficiently allocate money to borrowers on a basis of shared responsibility for risk.

8) *Will there be inflation?* No, because all money will be issued free of debt and interest.

9) *Will homeowners have to pay interest on their loans?* No, only a small handling fee will be payable, which will be used to defray the running costs of the system.

Frequently Asked Questions

10) *Will farmers be entitled to 0% loans?* Yes, loans will be available at 0% and will include the financing of crops. Only a handling fee will be levied.

11) *Will interest be payable on credit cards?* Once the new paradigm is in place the use of credit cards will be abolished and only debit cards will be available. Banks will charge a fraction of a percentage point for this service. Card holders will benefit from no longer having to pay interest and the large commissions which banks charge merchants.

12) *Will interest be paid on savings accounts?* Only nominal amounts of interest will be payable, as these savings will be backed 100% by the reserves of the deposit receiving bank. As inflation will be zero, cash held in savings accounts will retain its value.

13) *Will it be possible to earn a higher rate of interest elsewhere?* Yes, investment accounts will be available where it will be possible to earn a higher rate of interest. However, these investment accounts will not be entirely risk-free and the investor carries the risk that all or part of the capital invested may be lost.

14) *Will it be possible to repay the national debt?* Yes, the national debt will be repurchased and replaced with South African Notes at zero interest over a transitional period.

15) *Will there be taxation?* Taxation will be greatly reduced, as government and para-statals, for example, will no longer have to allocate vast sums of money for the payment of interest on their loans.

Index

A
ANC 16, 17, 55, 56, 61, 63, 64, 90, 121, 122
Anglo American Corporation 35
Atzmon, Gilad 70
Auschwitz 72, 73, 74, 75, 76, 77, 78, 83
Australian State Bank 25, 27

B
Bair, Sheila 98
Bank of England 13, 22, 29, 31, 45, 96, 102, 104, 105, 108, 109, 113, 116
Bank of North Dakota 112
Bankorp 96
Bank von Ernst 14, 49
Basic Law of 1949 58
Benson, Ivor 14
Beyers, Frederick William 24
Billiton, BHP 53
Bilateral Investment Treaty 58
Bletchley Park 74
Booysen, Steve 109
Botha, Barbara 49, 68
Botha, General Louis 19
Bouaerd, Michel de 72
Brown, Gordon Chancellor of the Exchequer 103, 104
Burnside, Duncan 37
Butcher, Willard C. 35

C
Carswell, Douglas 108
Central Reserve Bank 21, 26
Chamberlain, Houston Stewart 85
Chase Manhattan Bank 35
Chicago Plan 123
Christie, John 36
Churchill, Winston 30, 31, 74, 85, 119

Index

CIA 17, 93
CIEX 95
Committee on Currency and Banking 22
Crane Currency 62, 63, 64
Creswell, Colonel Frederic Hugh Page 13, 24, 25, 26
Curtis, Myles 62

D
Davel, Tom 65
De Beers Consolidated Mines 92
De Jongh, Dr Theunis 61, 93
De Klerk, State President Frederick Willem 14, 15, 49
De Lange, Johan 60
Deutsche Arbeitsfront (German Labour Front) 79
Diederichs, Dr Nico 13, 93, 94
Dr J. E. Holloway, 14
Du Toit, Adriaan 68
Dürr, Michael 57, 58, 89

E
Eisenhower, Dwight 74

F
Farben, I. G. 77
Faurisson, Professor Robert 83
Federal Reserve Bank 22, 36, 97, 101, 103, 107
Field, A.N. 28
Financial Services Authority 98
Finkelstein, Professor Norman 81

G
Galbraith, Kenneth 86, 87
Gauteng Law Society 66
Gauweiler, Peter 101, 102
General Mining 20
George, David Lloyd 84
George, Eddie Governor of the Bank of England 104
Germany 14, 28, 30, 31, 46, 47, 58, 63, 69, 70, 71, 73, 77, 78, 79, 81, 84, 85, 86, 87, 101, 102, 123

Gesiecke & Devrient 63
Gilbertson, Brian 53
Gini, Corrado 15
Gold Conference 22
Goldman Sachs 103
Gordon Institute of Business Science 112

H
Haft, Harry (Herschel) 77
Hawker, Dianne 59
Henderson, Senator Charles 42, 43, 45
Hertzog, J.B.M. 28
Hitler, Adolf 46, 47, 70, 71, 78, 79, 81, 84, 85, 87
Hofmeyr, Jan Hendrik 33
Holloway, Dr J. E. 14
Holocaust 67, 68, 69, 70, 72, 73, 74, 75, 77, 81, 82, 83
Horwood, Senator Owen 93
House of Commons 40, 108

I
IMF 17, 93, 123
Income Tax Act 19
International Jewish Sports Hall of Fame 77
International Reciprocal Trade Association 114
International Red Cross 75, 82
Ismail, Aboobaker 91

J
Jackson, Andrew 16
Jagger, John William 22, 24, 28

K

Kennedy, President John F. 87
King, William Lyon Mackenzie 33, 43, 44, 84
Krugerrands 64, 65

L
Labour Party 13, 22, 24, 25, 27, 29, 36, 37, 38, 39, 42, 43, 45

Index

Lange, Johan de 60
Laubsher, Gerhard 95
Leuchter, Fred 73
Ley, Dr Robert 79
Lincoln, President Abraham 40
London Interbank Offered Rate (LIBOR) 99

M
Madeley, Walter Bayley 27
Mail & Guardian 17, 67, 68, 84, 90, 117, 122
Marcus, Governor Gill 55, 56, 57, 59, 61, 62, 63, 64, 65, 66, 67, 68, 84, 89, 90, 91, 106, 107, 108, 117
Maré, Joseph 60
Maurice, Emil 79
Max Planck Institute 73
Mbeki, President Thabo 56
Mbhele, Musa 59, 60
Mboweni, Governor Tito 52, 54, 55, 56, 57, 66, 90
Merriman, John X 24
Miles, Professor David 113
Mminele, Deputy Governor Daniel 100
Mokate, Deputy Governor, Dr Renosi 61
Monetary Policy Committee 17, 113, 114, 133
Monetary Reform Act 125, 127, 137
Morgan, J. P. 97, 98, 99, 100, 103
Mushet, James Wellwood 24
Mvinjelwa, Andile 65
Myburgh, John 66

N
Nakache, Alfred 76, 77
Nettleton, Frank 25
New World Order 9, 16, 19, 93
Niemeyer, Sir Otto 45
Montagu Norman 29, 45, 116
Noseweek 96

O
Organisation for Cooperation and Economic Development 15

P

Payne, Albert 52
Pelt, Professor Robert van 83
Postmus, Dr J. 37
Pound, Ezra 110, 111
Project Hammer 95

R

Ralfe, Gary 92
Reichsbank 29, 31, 46, 79, 133
Relly, Gavin 35
Republic Broadcasting Network 17, 69
Reserve Bank of Australia 17, 60
Rhodes, Cecil John 20
Roberts, Dr Paul Craig 99
Rockefeller, David 93
Rothschild, Nathan 22
Rudolf, Germar 73
Russian Central Archives 73

S

Schacht, Dr Hjalmar 79
Scholz, Adolf Heinrich Wilhelm von 28
Second Bank of the United States 10, 16
Shamir, Yitzhak 81
Strakosch, Sir Henry (born Heinrich) 20, 24, 30, 31
Smit, Dr Robert 93
Smith, Senator Sidney 39
Smuts, General 19
South African Air Force 17, 91
South African Bank Note Company 59, 60, 61, 62, 63, 92
South African Free Market Foundation 52
South African Party 22, 24
South African Reserve Bank Act 48, 107, 125, 140
Sovereign Wealth Fund 17, 114
Stals, Chris 48, 54, 55, 95

T

Treaty of Westphalia 124

Index

Truman, Harry S. 74

U
UBUNTU Party 120, 121, 122
Union Corporation 20
United Nations 15
University of Stellenbosch 54
US Federal Energy Regulatory Commission 99
US Federal Reserve Bank 22, 35, 97, 101, 103, 107
US Justice Department 98

V
Vault, Slaughter and May 92
Vivian, Professor Robert 129

W
Walpole, Sir Robert 109
Wanless, Alexander 38
Wehrmacht 79, 80
Werth, Albertus 34, 35
Windsor, HRH the Duke of 87
Wood, US Brigadier General Robert E. 31

Z
Zulberg, Gary 61, 62
Zürich 13, 93, 95

For Product Safety Concerns and Information please contact our EU
representative GPSR@taylorandfrancis.com
Taylor & Francis Verlag GmbH, Kaufingerstraße 24, 80331 München, Germany

www.ingramcontent.com/pod-product-compliance
Lightning Source LLC
Chambersburg PA
CBHW050833160426
43192CB00010B/2009